PRAYER
GOD'S INVITATION
TO RELATIONSHIP

PAUL HOLT

WESTBOW
PRESS®
A DIVISION OF THOMAS NELSON
& ZONDERVAN

WestBow Press books may be ordered through booksellers or by contacting:

WestBow Press
A Division of Thomas Nelson & Zondervan
1663 Liberty Drive
Bloomington, IN 47403
www.westbowpress.com
1 (866) 928-1240

ISBN: 978-1-9736-4539-9 (sc)
ISBN: 978-1-9736-4541-2 (hc)
ISBN: 978-1-9736-4540-5 (e)

Library of Congress Control Number: 2018913486

Print information available on the last page.

WestBow Press rev. date: 02/08/2019

CONTENTS

ACKNOWLEDGEMENTS

I have read many books about prayer over the last fifty years and been greatly enriched. It is very likely that other authors may recognise their insights in this book. I have accredited as many as I have quoted but apologise for any omissions.

Many people have given me support and encouragement to complete this book. Rev Kip Crooks provided the opportunity to deliver this material in small group settings; Sam Radford and Robin Holt shared their enthusiasm for the project. Christina Parsons, Rev Julian Raffey and Ian McColl all read earlier drafts and made valuable suggestions. Thanks too to my wife Claire who proof-read the text and assisted in checking the references, and gave me great encouragement along the way. My grateful thanks also to Venus Gamboa and all the team at Westbow Press.

PREFACE

Many people are curious about prayer. Is it just about asking God to do something? Is there anything else to it? Why do some people seem to pray a lot while others seem to get on quite well without it?

Christians are especially encouraged to pray, yet many followers of Jesus struggle with it. Some may have given up praying by themselves because they found it too hard. Others may have become bored with individual prayer because it seems to be going nowhere. Maybe others have yet to start, but are put off by thinking they need to acquire a technical skill to get going. And there are those who say they would love to pray if only the situation was right, or they had enough time.

You may be inquisitive about prayer generally, or a bit dissatisfied with your own prayer life. Perhaps you are a church or study group leader looking for ways to help others explore the subject of individual prayer. If so, I hope that you will find in these pages resources to help and encourage. My own prayer is that God will use this book to inspire and refresh you in your relationship with Him through prayer.

How to Use This Book

This book has been written bearing in mind that many do not have much time to read. If you only have half an hour to spend, then pick any part and "dive in." It is not necessary to read each Chapter in order (although it helps).

Each Chapter ends with a summary, together with some prompts for reflection to help you think further. Individual prayer is of course an intensely practical activity - it involves *doing* things - so there is also a Prayer Toolbox at the end of each Chapter with hands-on suggestions for action. These can provide a basis for building a new (or renewed) prayer activity, and a focus for reviewing what may have gone well. In the end, of course, it is God the Holy Spirit who inspires us to pray, and teaches us what we need to learn.

If, having read this book, individual prayer seems like an adventure you want to be part of, it will have succeeded in its purpose.

INTRODUCTION

Prayer is for some a daily joy, for others it seems a chore. Others, again, are curious, or perhaps even mystified. The comment, "I really must get round to praying (or praying again)," expresses what many of us think from time to time.

Where would be the best place to start thinking about individual prayer? This book explores prayer as a response to the God who invites us into relationship. We can connect with Him and build that relationship through individual prayer, as we open the door of our inner selves to experience more of Him. Prayer understood in this way involves claiming time and space, listening as well as speaking, doing as well as receiving. God seeks us out and rejoices in our company, and as we respond through prayer, our relationship with Him grows.

God wants us to enjoy the good things He has for us through prayer. However, if we experience individual prayer as boring, tedious, and monotonous (or we stay at the "curious" stage), then it is likely that our ideas about it are too small. So how can we move on?

Moving Past the Blockage

If we are experiencing blockages in our desire to pray, such as thinking of prayer as a boring, empty religious obligation we are supposed to get on with, or feeling we just do not know where to start, our own efforts at trying harder may not get us far. There may need to be a different approach; we may need God to surprise us. Rather like the delicious aroma of food being prepared in the kitchen may excite our appetite, we need God first to refresh, enlarge, and enrich our view of Him and what it means to be His child, His friend. Again, just as the light must shine through the diamond first before its dazzling infinity of colour can be seen, we need God to enliven our limited notions of prayer with fresh energies of His own. We may then discover that we so *want* to spend time with Him in prayer and *enjoy* His company that we let nothing stand in our way.

If we really knew individual prayer as our opportunity to "make the God connection" (in Jo Saxton's phrase[1]), surely all boredom and dullness – or hesitation and uncertainty - would be drenched by the vivid colours of His glory. The richness of flavours of the Great Banquet He has prepared for those who follow Him would take us to new levels. Can we get to the place where our expectancy that God will meet us as we pray fills us with the excitement of anticipation?

In what follows, I invite you in Chapter One firstly to re-imagine individual prayer as one of the ways in which we can respond to God's invitation to relationship. Whether we experience this invitation as a joyful prompt, or more negatively as an inner prod, the Author is the same. We will see how setting out to pray individually requires some intentional preparation and planning on our part, and in Chapter Two we look at some of the steps that Jesus recommended to help us prepare to encounter the living God in the secret place of prayer.

Our developing relationship with God through prayer has many facets, rather like rich, diverse, and appetising food on the same plate, or colours from the same diamond. In this book, only a

---

[1] Jo Saxton, *Real God, Real Life,* (London: Hodder, 2010)

small selection has been made. Beginning in Chapter Three with the dimension of openness and honesty, emphasis is laid on the importance of keeping nothing from Him (in the light if His complete knowledge of us). Using examples from the Psalms known as Laments, we are encouraged to bring before God even our misgivings and disappointments about life.

Our human relationships teach us that listening is as important as speaking if our friendships are to grow. This also holds true for our relationship with God, thus the second facet of the prayer relationship – listening – is considered in Chapter Four. To prepare the ground for an encounter with Him in this way, we look at ways of listening *for* God as well as listening *to* Him, including meditation and prayerful, imaginative reflection on Scripture.

As our connection with God grows through prayer, there develops a 'transforming conversation' with Him (to use David Wilkinson's phrase)[2]. We explore this third facet of the prayer relationship with God in Chapter Five by looking at several examples where this transformation has taken place, including Bob Pierce (World Vision), Corrie Ten Boom (a survivor of the Holocaust), Amy Carmichael (a pioneering mission partner in India), and Beatrice Smith (who lived through the Rwandan genocide).

God chooses to extend His Kingdom in the world by means of a partnership with human beings. Scripture (and very many human stories) demonstrates that God calls individuals to work together with Him to bring about transformation – personal, cultural, national. One of the ways in which He does this is through people interceding for others in prayer. Thus in Chapter Six we consider the fourth and final facet (in this selection) of our prayer relationship with God – partnering through intercession. We consider how intercession can

---

[2] David Wilkinson, *When I Pray What Does God Do?* (Oxford: Lion Hudson, 2015)

build our relationship with God as we learn to share His priorities and pray for others according to His will. The Chapter concluded with a practical discussion around the importance of building and maintaining a structure in our intercessions.

God invites us to pray so that we may encounter Him, be open with Him, listen for Him and work with Him, to be part of the transformational change He seeks to bring. For our part, individual prayer is built into our day-to-day lives as part of a personal culture – the way we do things. Accordingly, in Chapter Seven we look at the importance of having a habit of prayer, and how we can go about building one.

The book ends as it begins with Jesus's famous invitation to all who hear Him knocking at the door of their hearts, that He will come in and share life with us. God invites; prayer is one way in which we respond,

> Listen! I am standing at the door and knocking; if you hear my voice and open the door, I will come in to you and eat with you, and you with me.[3]

My hope and prayer is that, as you read on, you may open the door wider to Jesus. I pray that God the Holy Spirit, who connects is with Jesus, will revitalise our imagination with a sense of vibrancy and excitement as we picture afresh what being a 'friend of God' could be like. We may start to think we really *want* to pray, *want* to be with Him, and receive the blessing He has for us.

---

[3] Rev 3:20

1

THE GOD WHO INVITES:
PRAYER AS RESPONSE

Most Christians would agree that praying by themselves –
individual prayer - is important, yet many of us struggle to make
it happen. We may imagine that we are not praying enough (as
though effective prayer could be measured in minutes or hours),
or that we are not praying properly (as though 'correct' words and
phrases were necessary). We hear about people who spend hours
in prayer, yet for some of us a couple of minutes a week is a stiff
challenge. I *ought* to pray more; we all *ought* to pray more yet the
reality may not measure up; a sense of discouragement around
prayer is often close at hand.

Others are fascinated by the idea of prayer, especially when thinking
of it as a way of connecting with God. We may be deeply affected
by the thought of being able to communicate with the One who
sustains the universe and yet is prepared to listen, to be available,
to mere human beings. And it is a fascination that does not seem
to go away.

Maybe there is a suspicion that praying in this way is only for
the "super-spiritual" or for those who have acquired the "knack."

Maybe we think our struggles arise because we are "not very good at praying" (or even, that we are not very good Christians). Despite the many helpful books and websites around about how to pray[4] and exhortations from Christian preachers that we should take our prayer lives more seriously, praying alone may become something that lives in the "too hard box" and looks like staying there.

Understanding the Purpose of "Ought"

In whatever way we think of prayer there may well remain that inward conviction that we *ought* to pray, like some inner pestering voice whose insistence we can never completely silence. But what does this mean for us? How can we understand what is going on?

Individual prayer works as a connection with God. If we have stopped praying (or have yet to start), we may experience inward prompts to pray. I am suggesting that these are rather like alarms sounding to let us know that we have yet to respond to God, who is inviting us to develop our relationship with Him. To explain this more fully, we need to go back to first principles. Christian faith proclaims that humans are here because God *wants* it that way. No matter how we may think of Creation in our scientific age, the story of human beginnings in Genesis describes a relationship with God broken by self-seeking and disobedience. Jesus – as God the Son - came to restore the relationship. He is looking for people who share His priorities, His passion for God's Kingdom, and who understand His heart - in short, to be His friends. He promises forgiveness, a new start, peace, and joy. The amazing truth is that God seeks us out to be in relationship with Him, and through the life, death, and resurrection of Jesus He has done everything necessary to bring that relationship into being – with

---

[4] I have listed at the back of this book some of the websites I have personally found useful.

one exception. There remains something only you or I can do, that is saying "Yes" to Him. If Jesus Christ is or has ever been a living Reality for us (no matter how dimly or infrequently), this is because at a deep level we have become conscious that He has called us into relationship. Individual prayer is our connection with God; it is how the relationship functions.

Relationship, not Religion

For followers of Jesus Christ, relationship with Him is primary. We see this right at the beginning of Jesus's earthly ministry. When Jesus called His original disciples the Gospel writer notes that "He called them to be with Him"[5], that is, to establish a relationship with Him, *before* He sent them out to do anything. Being comes before doing; it is relationship not religion.

Of course, the word "relationship" is used very widely to cover a whole range of associations between people; but fundamentally, two ideas are always in play when we talk of relationship, namely connectedness and intimacy. Psychologists tell us that we are built for relationship, and our emotional and physical health may suffer in the long term if we perceive ourselves to be alone.

Jesus once used a vivid image when He spoke of His relationship with believers. He said He was the "true vine,"[6] and went on to describe a key quality of this intimate and organic relationship as "abiding"; Him with us and us with Him,

> I am the true vine... Abide in me as I abide in you. Just as the branch cannot bear fruit unless it abides in the vine, neither can you unless you abide in me. I am the vine and you are the

---

[5] Mark 3:14
[6] John 15:1

branches. Those who abide in Me and I in them bear much fruit, because apart from Me you can do nothing... If you abide in Me and My words abide in you, ask for whatever you wish, and it will be done for you. My Father is glorified by this, that you bear much fruit and become my disciples.[7]

The image of a vine was especially significant for Jesus's first Jewish hearers. For example, in Old Testament prophecy[8] the nation of Israel is compared to a vine, planted by God. For us much later readers (perhaps without the specialist background), we still know that in order to produce the grapes that are made into wine, the branches need the most intimate connection possible with the vine stem if they are to remain alive, let alone produce grapes. Indeed, for Jesus, the state of abiding is the precondition for fruitfulness[9]. Jesus says that He becomes a part of us as we abide - remain, hold on to, stay - in Him. In other words, keeping Him close keeps our spiritual lives real.

The Holy Spirit and Relationship

Keeping someone close whom we have never seen may sound tricky (even if it is Jesus). In fact, Jesus spoke to His disciples about the importance of abiding in Him on the night before He died. Perhaps He knew that the disciples would be wondering how they could maintain their relationship with Him if He was shortly to be no longer with them. Jesus used this opportunity to talk about the Holy Spirit's role in maintaining the close connection with God. Jesus was very specific about how this works, and described three ways

---

[7] John 15:1, 4-5, 7-8.

[8] Isaiah 5:1

[9] In the New Testament, this word carries the sense of growing in relationship with Jesus and becoming more like Him.

in which the Holy Spirit engages with His followers[10]. Firstly, He is *with* us, in the sense that He is personally present and keeps company with us, walking beside us, as friends or family on a journey together. Secondly, He *abides* with us, that is He remains with us not only as our travelling companion but as One who will never go away. Finally, He is *within* us, a Presence of which we may be inwardly conscious, to feel inside. He is so close that it is even possible to grieve Him, literally to upset Him[11]. What the Holy Spirit does is personal; He reaches out to the person in us; He is "in our hearts."[12]

Jesus describes Him as "comforter" and "guide" - roles rooted in an understanding of Him as one who maintains the relationship with Jesus, across time and space. So we can expect that there will be occasions when He will make His presence especially felt in our inmost selves, especially if our prayer lives are losing their way. Although He does calm our fears, provide reassurance and consolation, we are apt to misunderstand and therefore limit His activity as "Comforter" if we only think in terms of a soothing Presence inducing cosy feelings of solace and relaxation. There is a famous example of a less-familiar form of comforting in a scene from the Bayeux Tapestry (the eleventh-century work of art depicting the Norman conquest of Britain), where a frame depicts King Harold comforting his troops by prodding them with a pike.

This may sound mysterious (indeed, God is deep Mystery) but means that at least we can expect to *feel* the Holy Spirit, to become aware of His influence in our motivations and desires from somewhere deep within. An old hymn puts it this way,

---

[10] John 14:16
[11] Ephesians 4:30
[12] Romans 5:5

And His that gentle Voice we hear, soft as the breath of even, that checks each fault, that calms each fear, and speaks of heaven.[13]

The Holy Spirit maintains our relationship with Jesus by inspiring us to pray, for prayer (personal as well as corporate) provides the connection with God. It is one of the ways in which we "abide" in Him. Prayer is the fabric of the relationship, a means by which we relate to Jesus Christ in intimacy and closeness.

Being Part of the Family

The vine, of course, has many branches. As followers of Jesus are abiding together in Him, a shared togetherness can result. Accordingly, St Paul develops these ideas of intimacy and connectedness in relationship with Jesus Christ by picturing a pattern of family relationships,

> You are in the Spirit, since the Spirit of God dwells in you. For all who are led by the Spirit of God are children of God... you have received a spirit of adoption. When we cry, 'Abba! Father!' it is that very Spirit bearing witness with our spirit that we are children of God.[14]

He uses the language of indwelling – "the Spirit of God *in* you", an inner recognition of a close and personal relationship that expresses itself in the language of family, where the word "Abba, Father" is an unforced and wholly natural expression of children's trusting love for their parent.

---

[13] Harriet Auber (1829)
[14] Romans 8:9, 14-16

Prayer as Thirst for God

We have seen how the Holy Spirit may prompt us if our individual prayer life is in difficulty, or we have yet to start. However, He may encourage us in other ways also. For example, most of us are familiar with desire – experienced as a wish, a want, a longing, a yearning perhaps. Frequently desire attaches itself to someone or something else, and we can spend a great deal of time and work to try and acquire what we think we want. However, things rarely work out as we had hoped. AS CS Lewis comments, we discover that something has evaded us in the reality and we are left with,

> ... the scent of a flower we have not found, the echo of a tune we have not heard, news from a country we have never yet visited.[15]

It is in the nature of "things" that they do not in the end satisfy at a deep and lasting level. It matters not whether those things are material possessions or human relationships: the power to satisfy completely and endlessly is simply not theirs. The disturbing realisation dawns that our desire has outstripped the opportunities available to satisfy it. What a wonderful relief (and surprise) to discover then that this is probably how God intended it to be. In His faithful, patient, and merciful persistence, He wants to keep us dependent on Him: to remind us that only He has the bread that satisfies all hungers, and the water that quenches all thirsts. As Maria Boulding, a contemporary Benedictine nun and deep thinker about God wrote,

> God creates in human hearts a huge desire and sense of need, because He wants to fill them with the gift of Himself.[16]

---

[15] CS Lewis, 'The Weight of Glory' in *Screwtape Proposes a Toast, and Other Pieces,* (London : Fount, 1993) 98
[16] Maria Boulding, *The Coming of God,* (London : SPCK, 1986) 1

An experience of longing for God may be part of the inward prompt to pray. Our thirst for a living, vibrant, dynamic relationship with Him is His way of reminding us that we are missing at His party, the *only* party that will entirely drench our longings in fulfilment.

So if we become conscious that our prayer life is flagging and we are rediscovering those "running on empty" feelings, we *recognise that those very feelings of emptiness, longing and thirst are aroused by God Himself.* In this way, we have the opportunity to go back to first principles and re-connect with Jesus; at this very place, He meets us with the living water of His Presence.

In summary, God invites us to share a relationship with Him. He knows this will be of the greatest blessing to us and, through us, outwards to the world (we are here for His purpose). If we are not giving the time and effort to respond to His invitation through individual prayer, then the Holy Spirit may use a prompt, a prod, a feeling of "ought" or even "running on empty." A verse in the Psalms puts it this way, "In very faithfulness Thou hast caused me to be troubled."[17]

If we understand this inner prompt that "we should be praying" as something from the Holy Spirit, a prod that awakes us from spiritual drowsiness, or a recognition of a thirst for Someone greater, where do we go next? Should our response be simply be variations on the theme of "trying harder," like striving to master a technique through self-improvement?

Individual Prayer – a Technical Skill?

One of the reasons some find praying by themselves hard (or are put off from starting at all) is the vague – but mistaken - idea that

---

[17] Psalm 119:75 *(Book of Common Prayer)*

they need a special skill to do it properly, like playing a musical instrument. In this case, someone spends time with a skilled teacher as part of the learning process. With practice, the student masters the skills and they become a proficient player. Importantly though, the goal of this learning is to make the student *independent* of the teacher. The day will come when the teacher has no more learning to impart, and the student is ready to stand on their own as a competent performer; the day of the last lesson will have come.

But prayer is very different. As Ruth Burrows in her book *The Essence of Prayer* reminds us, "prayer is not a technique, it is a relationship."[18] Prayer is not a practice to get right *for* God, something we learn to do independently of a relationship with Him. Prayer by contrast is the means by which we relate *to* God, the very process by which we are drawn closer together. Far from being a technique to get right, or a holy obligation that Jesus expects of us, devoid of life and passion, it is instead a secret space where we can connect with God. Through prayer, He can deepen His relationship with us. Rather like happiness, prayer is not a destination, it is a journey – a journey with God the Holy Spirit as our companion and guide, a presence and prompt, One who provokes and encourages.

One of the most poignant parts of the Genesis story of Adam and Eve's disobedience is the point where they discover shame. When God comes to the Garden in the cool of the evening they run away and hide. Missing them, God calls out "Where are you?"[19] We are created for relationship with God; He has taken the initiative to come and find us through the historical life of Jesus, His death and resurrection. His Presence remains with us through the Holy Spirit He has given us. So this inward prompt to pray, this "holy nudge", is highly likely to be the Holy Spirit's reminding us that we are somehow missing at the party. He is pointing us towards the

---

[18] Ruth Burrows, *The Essence of Prayer*, (London: Bloomsbury, 2016) 15
[19] Genesis 3:8,9

9

profound sense of rootedness that a relationship with Jesus brings (for life in Jesus is designed to be *good* news, sharing in His life is to have a part in His *joy* and rest in His *peace).* God delights in us, misses us and seeks our company, longing to give us more of Himself to enjoy. Maria Boulding sums up like this,

> We foolishly believe that prayer is about our own efforts. Our prayer is God's work, God's creation. As you kneel there, sit there … you are saying 'Yes' to God with your whole being to His Will that you should be, that you should be you, that you should be united to Him. Your prayer is God's word of longing and love in you, God's breathing of the Spirit in you, to make you want the union He wants. His desire is going through your heart to leap up to Him.[20]

SUMMARY

- God has made us to be in relationship with Himself;
- Maintaining the relationship is part of the Holy Spirit's ministry;
- Individual prayer is one of the forms in which we can respond to God's invitation to connect with Him (and enjoy the relationship).
- The relationship is realised and deepened through individual prayer. We breathe the atmosphere of Heaven.
- The invitation to pray – itself a work of God – is an invitation to draw closer to Him as He longs for us to be in closer relationship with Him.

We may experience His invitation perhaps as a prompt, or even a twinge of regret. Jesus's picture of Himself as the vine, with His followers as the branches, shows that connection and intimacy with

---

[20] Op. cit. 100

Jesus is before anything else we do as Christians; discipleship is about relationship rather than religion. The Holy Spirit, who does not leave us, is likely to prompt us to respond to God's gracious invitation of fellowship. St Paul's image of family makes the same point, that is, the Holy Spirit dwells within Christian disciples, convincing us we are children of God. We are like children who can enjoy a close, profoundly personal relationship with Him, and say "Abba" to their father.

REFLECTIONS

❖ If you have an inward prompt that you *ought* to pray, have you recognised this as a ministry of God the Holy Spirit to you?

❖ Does the recognition that God wants to be in a relationship with you change the way you feel about individual prayer? If so, how?

❖ Have you ever experienced an awareness of a "thirst for God?" How did it feel?

PRAYER TOOLBOX - 1

✓ How about doing a mental "stock-take" of how you feel about individual prayer? Have you found it bewildering, not knowing where to start, or have you tried it before and given up?

✓ Take a notebook and write down "where you are up to" with individual prayer, then refer to it at the end of each Chapter in this book and see if anything has changed. If so, make a note for future reference.

2

MEETING WITH GOD: PRAYER AS INTENTIONAL

We have been exploring the idea that individual prayer connects us with God. It is how we develop a friendship with Him. This relationship has many facets, four of which we will look at shortly, in particular openness, listening, transformation and partnering. To begin with, however, it will be important to consider some very down-to-earth, practical advice about praying, from none other than Jesus Himself. It might surprise us to think that Jesus had a habit of individual prayer; after all, He *was* God. While there is deep mystery here, clearly Jesus knew how important prayer was for maintaining a close and intimate relationship with His heavenly Father.

Jesus was very much a Man of prayer. The Gospels provide many examples where He prays. Only on a couple of occasions however does He teach *about* prayer[21]. One is recorded by Matthew's gospel as part of Jesus's Sermon on the Mount. He said,

> Whenever you pray, go into your room and shut the door and
> pray to your Father Who is in secret; and your Father who sees

---

[21] For example, the Parable of the Friend at Night (Luke 11:5-8), the Unjust Judge (Luke 18:1-8) and the Pharisee and the Publican (Luke 18:9-14)

in secret will reward you. When you are praying, do not heap up empty phrases as the Gentiles do; for they think that they will be heard because of their many words. Do not be like them, for your Father knows what you need before you ask Him.[22]

Jesus makes clear that prayer is the means of communicating with God. He packs four key instructions into three short verses as He shows us the essence of individual prayer.

'Whenever you Pray....'

Jesus never sought to persuade His followers to pray, or coax them into believing that individual prayer was a good idea. He gave no reasoned arguments for the importance of prayer. In this way He was following the assumptions of His first (Jewish) hearers; there was no sense of the permissive in the practice of prayer. Praying was simply something all believers did. In this sense there is some distance (and not just chronological) between them and us. As we know, some Christians seem to think of prayer – especially the individual kind – as optional, and not at all straightforward.

Maybe we need to re-focus on Jesus's assumptions about prayer. He *expects* that His people pray - prayer is a normal part of their everyday life. So if we are re-founding our prayer practice (or starting from scratch), perhaps the place to start is to refresh our recognition that *it is the regular thing to do*, as normal as eating and going to bed. But even if prayer is as unexceptional as the routine, run-of-the mill activities that sustain our daily life, nevertheless there needs to be an element of preparation. Jesus identifies four which, taken together, build up to an expectation of encounter – encounter with the Father "who sees in secret" and rewards those who seek Him. Prayer, despite its normality, requires *intentionality* – the time and the place need

---

[22] Matthew 6:6-8

to be claimed. Our prayer needs to be scheduled. Let us look at the four key preparatory steps.

Preparation for Encounter (1): "Go into your room"

Jesus says that before we pray, we are to seek a special place – "your room" – where "your Father, who sees in secret, will reward you." He may have been referring to an actual place, a physical location, but in any event, it will certainly be helpful for *us* to have somewhere specific in mind. It may be a very familiar place at home - your bedroom, study, den perhaps. "Your room" is likely to be full of the things that are important to you, maybe the place you go to for peace and refreshment, where you can be authentically yourself. Indeed, it may be a place where only the special people in your life are welcome. Why does Jesus suggest that it is in this deeply familiar place that we should prepare to meet Him, and not some other separate, holy place set apart for the purpose?

Jesus showed us the importance of being authentic in our individual prayer, that is, to be in our own place, to use "our own stuff", to share with God our own thoughts, needs, pains, and joys, to "keep it real." To pray in our room, in other words to be authentic in our prayer, means recognising that He is interested in everything about us, not just the religious bits or the nice bits or those things we may want to share. He will also be concerned with the dust under the bed (as it were), the things we may prefer to keep hidden.

Similarly, He wants us to go to our *own* room. This is especially important as we recognise that our Christian faith is designed to be worked out in the context of community, in fellowship and togetherness with other Christians. While we are often profoundly encouraged by fellow Christians, Jesus's words about praying in our own room means being ourselves with Him, giving full weight and recognition to our own perceptions and realities. It will also include not comparing ourselves adversely with others and drawing negative conclusions, like for example our faith may not seem as strong as another's, or we are not "as good" as they are. This kind of comparison is unnecessary and misleading. Jesus is not interested in how we might compare with other Christians; He is much more concerned with our following *Him*. Remember how He told Peter not to be diverted by wondering about another's discipleship? [23] While He is deeply committed to all, Jesus is uniquely faithful to you and me. Being in your own room, being authentic in prayer arises from your own personal relationship with Jesus, not out of trying to imitate someone else's.

To "go into your own room" draws a word-picture of intentionally claiming a space for individual prayer, the intimate, secret place, where we are most authentically ourselves. Jesus seeks to meet us there.

Preparation for Encounter (2): "Shut the door"

The action of door shutting implies a desire to shut out any potential distractions (as well as shutting ourselves in). It also shows an intention to concentrate, to mark out secluded space where we have opportunity to do and say what will not be seen or heard by others. We know it was Jesus's habit to go away by Himself and pray. He knew first-hand the blessing of communing with God in solitude. He bids us "shut the door" so we can be alone in that intimate, secret place, and enjoy the presence of God through individual prayer.

---

[23] John 21:21-22

Preparation for Encounter (3): "Pray to your Father..."

Who we think God is and what we imagine Him to be like has the most profound influence on what we say to Him in prayer. The Pharisees embellished their prayers with all kinds of external excellence because they thought of God as the supreme lawgiver who required scrupulousness in every detail. This replaced for them any notion of spontaneity, intimacy, or closeness. They missed the point that above all, God seeks not some technical, doctrinal accuracy in the words used but truth in the inward places. He is looking upon the intention of the heart.

John Eldredge in his book *Beautiful Outlaw* puts it this way,

> The point is not the words; the point is the fruit, their effect. Stained-glass language reflects a view of what Jesus is like; it shapes our perceptions of him and, therefore, our experience of him. [It] ...keeps Jesus at a distance, the polar opposite of the intimacy his entire life was committed to. It makes it hard to love him. This stuff actually gets in the way of loving Jesus. Listen— you can honour him, respect him, insist that others do, and never actually love Jesus. This is not what he wanted.[24]

So it is worthwhile pausing to consider how the words we use shape the God-reality for us. Even if we do not imagine God as old, benevolent and white-bearded (as some people evidently do), it is unlikely we will have no image *at all* as we pray. For example, when we call Him "Father," do we think of Him as some kind of a "divine parent" (a "good" or "bad" one)? Have we dressed Him up with clothes that do not fit Him, drawn not from how Jesus showed Him to be but instead from our own desires or fears?

---

[24] John Eldredge, *Beautiful Outlaw*, (London: Hodder, 2011) 144

No "Idols"

We may recall that the Israelites on their journey to the Promised Land were told not to make a "graven image" of God (a prohibition that formed the second of the Ten Commandments). The phrase "graven image" suggests a figure made by hand that is supposed to represent the one being worshipped. These days we are far less likely than the Israelites in the Old Testament to be sitting down with a block of wood (or a pile of gold) and chiselling out a god-like figure (or making a golden calf) to kneel before and worship. But the tendency to create idols remains. Some have made god into a fearsome, retributive tyrant who is never satisfied and seems endlessly content with creating guilt feelings amongst his followers. Others have made a god who is chiefly concerned with promoting happiness in his followers, and that the pursuit of happiness is the all-embracing priority (provided perhaps we don't do anyone any harm on the way).

Why should this be such an offence to God? There are many reasons but one stands out; an idol represents an attempt to replace Truth with a lie. When we start to substitute the True, imageless God who was fully revealed in Jesus with one of our own making, we limit and distort Him and start attributing to Him characteristics we may prefer (or may actually fear). Many will be familiar with C.S.Lewis' book *The Lion, the Witch and the Wardrobe*[25]. In the early part of the story, the children know Aslan the lion (who stands as an allegory for Jesus) as very warm and compassionate, gentle and caring. Yet, as the White Witch discovered, he had a terrifying and stern side. We must always remember, as Mrs Beaver said talking of Aslan, that he was a *wild* Lion. Jesus (like Aslan) will not be limited by our imaginations or tamed by our current understandings.

---

[25] C.S. Lewis, *The Lion, the Witch and the Wardrobe*, (London: Geoffrey Bles, 1950)

Jesus's first hearers would not have been surprised by His use of *Father* language in connection with God. The Old Testament (which is they would have known well) had many references to God as "Father" in a collective sense. What would have surprised them however is Jesus's characteristic way of speaking of *"my* Father." So when He speaks of "our" Father, it is a collective of personal relationships with the One Father. For example, in a family with a number of brothers or sisters, the dad is uniquely father to each of them as individuals, as well as being father to them all. Thus each child could truthfully speak of its father as "my dad." So Jesus – more aware than we can ever be of the deep Mystery of the Fatherhood of God - spoke of God as One who is in intimate connection with us, as (*y)our* Father.

As part of "shutting the door" as we prepare to pray, we may need to ask the Holy Spirit to cleanse our imagination of every distortion of God, and open the way for Him to encounter us in tenderness and truth.

Preparation for Encounter (4): The Secret Place

When you or I are in our room with the door shut, as we prepare to pray there is no one else there but God. He meets us in this secret place. The true Father God with whom we have to do and who calls us into fellowship with Him asks us to be honest with Him. This stems from what He already knows about us, a recognition that comes out in a familiar prayer,

> Almighty God, to whom all hearts are open, all desires known, and before whom no secrets are hid...[26]

We will be looking at openness before God in the next Chapter when we consider the importance of honesty in individual prayer, but for

---

[26] The Collect for Purity, *Book of Common Prayer*

now, it is enough to be reminded that God is deeply familiar with the secret places in our lives, and knows all about us. For example,

> For it was You Who formed my inward parts, You knit me together in my mother's womb. My frame was not hidden from You, when I was being made in secret.[27]

"Keep It Real"

God is not interested in pretence; He looks for the "truth in our inward being." [28] He is not taken in by our attempts to cover up or lie to ourselves. Like the adult at a kids' game of hide and seek, He knows exactly where we are, even though we may think our attempts at hiding have been successful. He knows all about us, even those things we may not yet already know about ourselves. Importantly, He is not just concerned about sinfulness. He will be the first to applaud our successes and faithfulness, Most graciously, He does not condemn, He does not berate or castigate; He does not delight in "rubbing our noses in it." Where there is sin, He simply bids us to go and have done with sin. There is no condemnation; He has already paid the cost of forgiveness.

Jesus tells us not to "heap up empty phrases," when we pray. If we find ourselves readily using words that have no real meaning for us (even if they are "religious" words), the words will become a smoke-screen between us and God. This does not mean that we avoid using formal prayers or the words of others when we pray. The point is that we should be on the lookout for substituting second-hand or empty, pious phrases for real communication with Him. Indeed, even without a prayer book, our prayers can become very formulaic. For example, we can catch ourselves saying the same

---

[27] Psalm 139:13,15
[28] Psalm 51:6

thing to Jesus yesterday as we did last week and a year ago – "please bless my family, bless our church, bless our clergy, bless my friends, etc." There is nothing wrong with praying for blessing but this can become just as much an empty formula as any repetition of phrases found in books of formal prayers.

Prayer is empty unless we have made it our own. Eloquence and earnestness are *not* the hallmarks of genuine prayer. In prayer we enter God's Presence, and He would have us be ourselves before Him. He wants us to "keep it real."

And this means work.

"Your Father Knows What You Need."

Prayer is always telling God what He already knows. So why pray? Simply because God has designed prayer to be a far richer experience for the disciple than simply presenting Him with a shopping list. When we pray for ourselves, we tell Him what we need; when we are interceding we tell Him what the world needs, but not out of a perception that He does not already know. On the contrary, prayer is about *sharing* with Him our concerns and using the opportunity to know more about *His* concerns and *our* opportunities to make a difference in His Name. In these ways, individual prayer develops the connectedness and intimacy that lie at the heart of relationship.

To conclude: in Matthew 6 Jesus gives us four very practical steps within His understanding of individual prayer (before teaching what we know as the Lord's Prayer). He is saying we need to get ourselves properly prepared, as it were to arrange the mental furniture, before we can fully enjoy His Presence in prayer.

SUMMARY

Jesus provided some basic advice about praying individually:

- "Go into your room"- find that personal space where we can be entirely ourselves with Him.

- "Shut the door"- close our minds to distraction and give ourselves space to concentrate.

- "Pray to your Father" - consider how we picture God as Father, especially notice with what clothes we may be using to dress the Invisible God. We may often need to cleanse our picture of the God we cannot see and ensure our imagination of what He is like conforms to Jesus Christ. How we think of Him will influence hugely the way in which we relate to Him in individual prayer.

- "The Secret Place" – free from any attempts to play 'let's pretend' or 'hide and seek' with God, He is the God who sees in secret, and invites us to keep our relationship very real with Him in prayer.

- God already knows what we need before we ask - individual prayer is never about telling God anything He does not already known (or may have forgotten).

- Instead, individual prayer is the connection with God. The blessing of relationship flows along this the spiritual channel.

REFLECTIONS

❖ How far does Jesus's instruction on individual prayer compare with your own approach to prayer?

❖ How comfortable do you feel with the knowledge that Jesus knows everything there is to know about you?

❖ How do you feel about the insight that Jesus knows what you need before you pray?

PRAYER TOOLBOX – 2: 'ENCOUNTER'

✓ "Go into your room" – Jesus seeks an authentic encounter with you, in your place, in an intentional space.

✓ "Shut the door" – seek some time and space where you and Jesus can be alone together.

✓ "Pray to your Father" – we may need to cleanse and re-claim the mental image of the One who bids us pray.

✓ "The Secret Place" – whether this is physical or mental, the secret place is where He seeks an encounter with us.

✓ "Your Father knows what you need" – we need not waste empty or flowery words with Him. He seeks our trust, openness, and genuine desire to be with Him.

3

Openness with God: Prayer as Honesty

We have been thinking about individual prayer as a way of connecting with God, and taking account of Jesus's real-world guidance about how to set about it. So far so good, but maybe some are now thinking: "okay, I recognise the potential of individual prayer for meeting with God, I've found my 'secret place' and I'm ready... but how can I get started?"

Getting Over the Threshold

We may need to navigate a "threshold" issue, something that needs to be named and resolved before we can get started. For example, the idea that the God of the Universe is somehow available in prayer is a source of deep awe and wonderment for some, but for others it also overwhelming. Another group may be held back by a sense of not knowing what to say. Thankfully, God the Holy Spirit helps us to pray, providing us with an inner assurance that we really *are* God's children, and He understands. As St Paul wrote,

For we do not know how we ought to pray, but that very Spirit intercedes with sighs too deep for words. And God, who searches the heart, knows what is the mind of the Spirit, because the Spirit intercedes for the saints according to the will of God.[29]

Many find that consciously inviting the Holy Spirit to make Himself known right at the start of the prayer time provides a sense of inner freedom and release, and helps them over the threshold into the sunshine of His Presence.

Openness – the Next Step

If any relationship is to be authentic, genuine and "the real deal," there is a need for honesty. No relationship can thrive on subterfuge, disguise, or any pretence that gets in the way of a real and sincere encounter. If this is true at a human level, how much more so must this be the case for our relationship with Jesus Christ? If individual prayer is to help us deepen our relationship with Him, we need openness, frankness, and honesty. We are not to play hide and seek with Jesus. We recall how He wants us to "go into your room and shut the door," to be authentically ourselves in our own space with Him. This "being ourselves" with Jesus can be both releasing yet deeply challenging.

On a human level, we are sometimes very hesitant to say what we really think, for fear of causing upset, or bringing about disapproval (or at worst, complete rejection). These cautions are important in their context, but there are limits on their usefulness when it comes to individual prayer. Unlike a human relationship, even the very best ones, Jesus knows everything there is to know about us from the outset. We do not need to disclose gradually to Him, imagining we must spare His feelings. There is a need to acknowledge to Him

---

[29] Romans 8:26-27

exactly the way it is, to be completely truthful with Jesus, so that our relationship with Him can deepen. It may seem like taking a risk with Him in being frank and open, yet on a human level many can witness to the release we experience in a friendship when we know that the other person really understands us and how we feel. We find that the risk was worth taking. How much more so with Jesus: He would have us talk to Him in our own authentic voice, holding nothing back. Perhaps this is one reason why we are told not to use empty phrases in His presence, or to hide behind conventional religious phrases. Prayers that others have prepared can often provide a rich source of inspiration and help us to overcome any difficulty we may experience in getting started in prayer. However, stock prayers, while being easy to repeat, can so easily become empty of either intention or meaning if we repeat them "parrot fashion."

"Owning Up"

Part of being fully open with Jesus inevitably involves us in some form of confession. Using this word may prompt some immediately to think of a formal occasion, where they tell God what has gone wrong while a priest listens. However, I am not here referring to Sacramental Confession, helpful though it can be. Instead, I want simply to emphasise that an essential part of meeting Jesus in the secret place of prayer is owning up about those motivations, desires, and real-life actions that damage others – in other words, sin. As we seek to be open with Jesus in prayer our understanding of sin will deepen. It is likely we will acquire a more dynamic understanding than simply "things I do wrong," to the point where it will embrace anything (including thoughts, tendencies, behaviours) that impairs, weakens or simply gets in the way of our relationship with Jesus

Where do we start? To begin with, we must never let ourselves think that we have no sin to confess. St John wrote that we are deceiving ourselves if we think this is the case. [30] Conscience helps us here, of course, but this is not infallible (a point discussed later). Even if we are aware of our own sin, that awareness itself may be warped. For example, someone may say, "I never do anyone any harm," or "I always try to do the right thing," unintentionally perhaps substituting their own yardstick for God's.

THE ROLE OF CONSCIENCE

A twentieth-century saint, Dr Sangster, encouraged all Christians to undertake what he termed a "spiritual check-up." His wisdom is equally relevant for today as we consider what is involved in confession. We may begin with conscience, that capacity for self-awareness that is one of the characteristics of being human. While it is often helpful to start here, those with much experience in walking the spiritual path advise us to be careful. Our consciences can be fallible. Due to our conditioning and experiences, it is likely that our consciences will be very alert and sensitive to particular behaviours while on the other hand being much less sensitive to others. Our consciences may be over-anxious and indeed, condemning, even when Jesus Himself is not. St John points out that God is greater than our consciences (especially when they condemn us), for He knows everything.[31]

We will become more acutely aware of what Jesus wants us to be like as we spend time with Him in individual prayer. This may involve some pain as we realise that what we are doing or planning may not be what God wants for us.

Studying Jesus in the Gospels and praying that He will teach us His ways is one of the most effective ways of educating our minds,

---

[30] 1 John 1:9
[31] 1 John 3:20

creating the circumstances for the kind of transformation that the Holy Spirit brings about as we concentrate on Jesus.[32] We know that the four Gospels provide many examples of Him at work, as well as selection of His parables[33]. As we read them we can build up a picture of Him, what mattered to Him, how He dealt with situations. God's aim for us, after all, is that we should come to be like Jesus. Sin is anything that gets in the way of this dynamic process, which is inspired and overseen by the Holy Spirit, and takes place in the context of relationship. As St Paul wrote,

By faith in Christ you are in direct relationship with God.[34]

JESUS REVEALS THE CHARACTER OF GOD

Looking at Jesus's instructions for individual prayer in the last Chapter, we saw how He used the title "your Father" when referring to God. We saw the importance of picturing God as Jesus showed Him to be, rather than any invention of our own (or someone else). This is especially important when it comes to owning up to God. Above all else, Jesus revealed the God who is love. The four Gospels give us many pictures of Jesus's love in action. Other New Testament passages will also help us. For example, St Paul had a vivid personal experience of God's love for him, and his famous poem about love (extensively used in church wedding services) draws on a multitude of Old Testament references to God, which Jesus personified. To make this point more vividly, in the following quotation I have substituted the word "God" for St. Paul's use of "love,"

---

[32] Romans 12:1-2

[33] It is important to remember that each Gospel does not contain every parable.

[34] Gal. 3:26 (*The Message*)

God is patient, *God* is kind; ... *God* does not insist on His own way, *God* is not irritable or resentful; *God* does not rejoice in wrongdoing, but rejoices in the truth. *God* bears all things, believes all things, hopes all things, endures all things.'[35]

We notice especially that God does not rejoice in wrongdoing; He does not tot-up our scores. It is a great sadness to encounter Christians who deep down suspect that God is the ultimate spoiler, the great "scold," the one who is never satisfied and always on the look-out for faults. For some it seems that God's chief joy is to make us feel guilty. Who would want to be open and honest before such a tyrant? How much this false god, this idol, needs to be dethroned in our lives and replaced by the True God that Jesus revealed. A great Victorian hymn (but still so relevant today) put it this way,

> For the love of God is broader than the measures of man's mind;
> And the heart of the Eternal is most wonderfully kind.
> But we make His love too narrow by false limits of our own;
> And we magnify His strictness with a zeal He will not own.[36]

It is, after all, as George Herbert wrote, "Love bade me welcome."[37]

When we are owning up to God, our mental picture of the one we are talking to needs to be based entirely on Jesus, God the Son, and the character of God the Father Whom He showed.

THE IMPORTANCE OF KNOWING FORGIVENESS

What next? The importance of absolution, of *knowing yourself to be forgiven* cannot be over-estimated. Some Christians are great at

---

[35] 1 Corinthians 13:4-7
[36] F. W. Faber (1814-1863)
[37] George Herbert (1593-1633) *Love (III) The Complete Poem,* ed. John Tobin (London: Penguin, 1991)

the confessing bit, but never listen for the word of forgiveness. They still labour under a sense of failure and guilt. In some Christian traditions, spoken words of Absolution, following a corporate act of confession, are an integral part of the worship service. Additionally, we may have a particularly favourite word of Jesus, such as "Go... and do not sin again,"[38] (as He said to the woman caught in adultery). Whatever words we use or hear the message remains the same,

> There is therefore no condemnation for those who are in Christ Jesus.[39]

We must never forget, as Ruth Burrows puts it, that God's love is "always on tiptoe to forgive."[40]

Honesty with the One Who Searches the Heart

So far we have been thinking about the things that impair our relationship with Jesus, the sin that comes to mind when we start being open, honest, and as transparent as we can with God. But of course, sin is not the only thing there is to find.

When we are seeking to be open with God in prayer, what happens may sometimes surprise us. For example, when we are at rest before God in the secret place, with no agenda, asking Him to lead us, into our minds may come unexpected thoughts, memories, feelings perhaps from way back. These are of a different order than the common, distracting thoughts that come across our minds when we are quiet that need gently setting aside (such as 'When will I do the housework?', 'Have I got my cousin's birthday card?'). Instead, these unanticipated thoughts are often accompanied by an emotional

---

[38] John 8:11
[39] Romans 8:1
[40] Ruth Burrows, *The Essence of Prayer*, (London: Bloomsbury, 2006) 23

intensity and can change the way we feel. How may we understand what is going on? It may well be that God, who seeks us out and searches our hearts,[41] is looking to take us deeper in our experience of Him.

Of course, no one would begin to claim they could stand over God's shoulder and watch Him at work (we are warned that His ways are not ours), nevertheless there are some clues arising from what may happen next. For example, my friend Charles was waiting quietly on God in prayer one day and into his mind came the pictorial memory of a friend he had not been in touch with for a long while. As Charles considered the memory of his friend's face, he also became aware of pain, deep down inside. Gradually the memory came back of a time when there had been deep hurt in their relationship: an argument got out of hand, harsh words were said, but the friend moved away shortly afterwards, they lost touch, and the memory receded. Charles began to feel that maybe God wanted him to sort this out and seek mutual forgiveness and reconciliation with his friend. Eventually he sought an opportunity to re-connect and, to his amazement, found that his friend had frequent and acute regrets over the incident. He too had been praying for an opportunity to put things right, and in this, God was glorified. Through these times of quiet waiting on God He can do His work with us, drawing us closer to Himself as (in this example) we are prompted to forgive and so help set others free.

Angry with God?

Is there anything else God might find as His Spirit searches our hearts? It may be that we are a bit short on holy thoughts, the wells of thankfulness may seem to have dried up, and praise has fallen silent. Instead, there may be sullenness, a sense of unfairness, even

---

[41] Jeremiah 17:10

anger or hostility towards God. Many Christians become deeply uncomfortable at the thought there may be anything else in their hearts towards God than thankfulness and praise, yet at the same time wonder why their prayers have gone dead on them.

Some may consciously suppress and try to hide any negativity towards God. Take, for example, the Christian widower whose wife had been in much pain for some time before she died from a distressing illness. He delights that she is now in glory and he praises God that she has been healed from her suffering and pain. Yet he struggles with loneliness, he pines for her company, and feels cheated of the years of companionship and shared joys they might have shared together. If he finds it too difficult to be open with God about the pain and the anger he feels, he will miss the blessing of knowing himself to be understood and accepted by God. Similarly, as we tap into our news feeds from internet, newspaper or radio, we may quietly seethe at the pain and distress, exploitation and greed, war and famine going on in the world. Maybe some secretly wonder who really *is* in charge and question how far God does rule. How we need to bring this passion, negative or positive, into our prayer and be open with God. There is no need to protect God from knowing the full extent of our negativity; indeed, what sort of protection do we think God needs?

On these occasions, we may therefore find ourselves more closely allied with what Gordon Mursell describes as the "prayer of protest."[42] He reminds us that saints from an earlier age have trodden this very path before us and left their thoughts in a group of Psalms that scholars distinguish as "Laments." Many speak powerfully and authentically from the secret place of prayer. For example,

---

[42] Gordon Mursell, *Out of the Deep, Prayer as Protest*, (London: Darton, Longman and Todd, 1989)

> Why, O Lord, do you stand far off? Why do you hide Yourself in times of trouble?... Why do the wicked renounce God, and say in their hearts, "You will not call us to account?"[43]

> How long, O Lord? Will you forget me forever? How long will you hide your face from me? How long must I bear pain in my soul, and have sorrow in my heart all day long?[44]

There are other examples where individual Psalms speak from a place of pain or distress, even a sense of abandonment by God. Some even complain that God has either forgotten or lost His power[45]. Consider,

> Be gracious to me, O Lord, for I am in distress. My eye wastes away from grief, my soul and my body also. For my life is spent with sorrow, and my years with sighing; my strength fails because of my misery, and my bones waste away.[46]

Psalm 88 encapsulates a sense of abandonment by God and isolation from friends and family,

> I'm standing my ground, God, shouting for help, at my prayers every morning, on my knees each daybreak. Why, God, do you turn a deaf ear? Why do you make yourself scarce?... the only friend I have left is Darkness.[47]

Psalm 74 - another lament Psalm – might be prayed with passion and tears by Christians today who are persecuted for their faith and have witnessed the destruction of their places of worship by anti-Christian militants,

---

[43] Psalm 10:1,13.
[44] Psalm 13:1-3
[45] Psalm 77:10
[46] Psalm 31:9-10
[47] Psalm 88:13-14, 18 (*The Message*)

Direct your steps to the perpetual ruins; the enemy has destroyed everything in the sanctuary. Your foes have roared within your holy place; they set up their emblems there. At the upper entrance they hacked the wooden trellis with axes, and then with hatchets and hammers, they smashed all its carved work. They set your sanctuary on fire...they burned all the meeting places of God in the land. We do not see our emblems; there is no longer any prophet, and there is no one among us who knows how long... Why do you hold back your hand; why do you keep your hand in your bosom?[48]

The Psalms of Lament remind us that the human condition remains very alike from age to age, and we may make them powerfully our own when our experience is similar. Similarly, of course, they also remind us that God's Presence is equally constant, and that this provides us with the continuing grounds for hope.

The story that follows illustrates very profoundly the decisive difference that being open with God at a time of darkness can make.

A hospital chaplain told me about a young girl suffering with leukaemia; she was a naturally positive and up-beat child, her parents were similar, and they had all done their best to keep her spirits up during her long stays in hospital and the various treatments she underwent. They, and all their friends, also prayed. As time went by it became clear that the child was very ill and unlikely to recover. The time for her birthday was coming close, and the family made careful preparations for this special day, including a birthday cake, of her favourite kind with the special icing she loved. The family arrived at the hospital with the cake and the makings of a little party to be greeted with the news they had dreaded for so long: the little girl had died just a half-hour before. The chaplain was in the ward, and was soon deeply involved with the tears and the heartbreak. A little later,

---

[48] Psalm 74:3-11

he asked the parents what they would like to do with the cake, and the father in his anger and his tears said, "I'd like to throw this cake in the face of God." The chaplain invited them to come with him to the chapel, bringing the cake. Once there – standing before the little altar with the brass cross upon it – he said, "This is as near as we're likely to come to God just now, so this would be a good place to throw the cake." The father picked up the cake, stood back, and hurled it at the cross, and amongst the sponge cake, the jam and the icing dripping from the altar both mum and dad broke down and wept and wept until no more tears would come.

There was a sequel to this story. The parents had had what is sometimes called a "conventional" faith up to this point, but from then on they spoke of a deepening awareness of God's Presence with them in their pain and loss. They gradually came to a place where their huge sense of anger and bereavement was suffused with a knowledge that God really was there and could be trusted to take all their negativity and gradually turn it towards His glory, all the time drawing them closer to Himself.

God searches the hearts, and it is unlikely that all He finds there will be flattering to us. Yet the knowledge that He is not remotely surprised or disappointed by what He has seen there somehow draws us into the renewal and transformational change He longs to bring. The knowledge of His loving and healing presence in those places can gradually free us from the negative effects of past hurt and damage. He has no use for an association with us built on conventional niceties or superficiality (no matter how Christian the words and phrases we use may sound). He does not want us to cover up in front of Him in our prayer. He wants us to "keep it real," for only then can He refresh us with streams that break out in the desert places.

Hannah's Prayer

One way of bringing these various aspects of honesty and openness in prayer together is to look at the Prayer of Hannah, recorded in the Old Testament.[49] Hannah was married and living in a time when fertility and large families were seen as a sure sign of God's blessing. Hannah's apparent inability to bear a child was not only grievous for her, but also made her the object of scorn and ridicule. She was laughed at and bullied by a fellow family member and carried a deep sense of personal failure, which the devoted love of her husband could not make up for. One day she went to the Temple, and there she prayed. She "poured out her grief to God" in deep distress, praying silently, just moving her lips, all the time weeping bitterly. When challenged by the elderly priest, Eli, and accused of drunkenness, she explained simply and without rancour that she had been "praying out of the fullness of grief and misery."[50]

We notice that Hannah knew where to take her profound sorrow and unmitigated distress. Rather like when a young child in a trusting relationship with their parents breaks their heart in tears to them as they explain what has gone wrong and why they are so sad, Hannah takes her pain and sadness to the One she knows will understand. She was entirely open with God, and held nothing back, spilling out in her prayer all the passion and emotion that her broken heart held. She demonstrates that God can be trusted to "take" all the messy, broken bits that go to make up our lives, all the intense feelings that are just too raw to think away or tame into obedient silence. However, as we read on in the story we observe that a change comes over Hannah as she completes her prayer. She has "something to eat, and is no longer downcast."[51] Sure, she has asked God for a child,

---

[49] 1 Samuel 1:1-19
[50] 1 Samuel 1:16 (NEB)
[51] 1 Samuel 1:16 (NEB)

that she may know the joy of pregnancy and childbirth, but she has evidently not received any assurance that this will in fact happen. Instead, after an early rise the next morning, she packs up the tents and heads back with her family to the village in the hills where they all live. We are not told how long after this Hannah and her husband made love, only that when they did, "God remembered her" and she later conceived. Their son was, of course, Samuel, one of the greatest heroes of faith in the Old Testament.

What are we to make of the change that came over Hannah? She was sobbing, distraught, sorrowing, and anguished but after she had prayed she was "no longer downcast." Elsewhere there are examples of people who pour out their distress and difficulty as to God in prayer as Hannah did. Similarly they find peace and a basis for hope, but not because of a change in their outward circumstances. Instead a change has come *in their perspectives,* the way they see their problems and difficulties. For example, the Psalmist having explained to God how low, depressed and discouraged he feels, goes on shortly afterwards to exclaim,

> Why are you so cast down, O my soul, and why are you so disquieted within me? Hope in God, for I shall yet praise Him, my help and my God.[52]

Perhaps the very act of letting it all go in prayer with the God who is love gives space for a deeper recognition that He simply *is,* and stands both within and beyond our pain.

His arms are wide enough to gather in and help us contain what is so hard. He gives us strength to get in touch with His deeper reality, where He can transform our sorrow, or anger, or pain with His comfort and grace. His Presence, indeed, is salvation.

---

[52] Psalm 42:5

37

SUMMARY

Individual prayer can develop our relationship with God in at least four ways:

- Openness and honesty,
- Engagement and listening,
- Transformed outlook,
- Partnering.

In this Chapter, we have considered openness and honesty.

The thought of being open with God in an attitude of honesty may at first seem very disturbing; we may even feel the need to keep some of ourselves back from Him, or at least hidden, especially the darker sides. What we imagine Him to be like, and how He is towards us, on may need some looking at as we seek to be open with Him. Jesus especially emphasised that God is Love.

We "own up" to our failures and shortcomings as part of this, so that the *blessing of His forgiveness and personal acceptance* may become real for us. If we own up only partially, or if we only give a little of ourselves away to God, there is only a little space for His blessing to fill. Similarly, owning before Him those other darker sides is vital if we are to have a relationship based in reality, including feelings of anger or even despair. For example, many of the Lament Psalms speak from the heart to God out of dark places, such as feelings of abandonment by God, or even downright despair at His apparent inactivity in the face of gross injustice. Even if there may be little else in our hearts but anger towards Him, our prayers will go dead on us if we do not trust Him enough to bring this forward in prayer. We can trust in His supreme tenderness for us.

REFLECTION

❖ How do we *really* feel about God? Is He "wonderfully kind" in our imagination (as that old hymn puts it)?

❖ Are we hiding anything from God, perhaps negative feelings towards Him?

❖ Do we need to ask Him to deepen our trust so we can be truly open with Him about what we *really* feel?

❖ Is His forgiveness and personal acceptance a reality for us?

PRAYER TOOLBOX – 3: BEING 'HONEST' IN PRAYER:

✓ Start praying by inviting God the Holy Spirit to help. He knows our weakness and intercedes for us in such a way that words are often unnecessary.

✓ Ask God to help us imagine Him as He is, as Jesus showed Him to be (and not as any lesser god we may have made up).

✓ Focus on Jesus, not ourselves.

✓ Tell Him how it *really* is.

✓ Ask Him to reveal what is getting in the way of our individual relationship with Him (i.e. sin) so we can own up to it.

PRAYER TOOLBOX – 3: BEING 'HONEST' IN PRAYER (Continued):

✓ Claim our forgiveness *and* acceptance. Revel in the truth that *"There is no condemnation for those who are in Christ Jesus."*

✓ Never be afraid to trust Him with everything, for He searches the hearts and looks for a relationship with Him based on openness

4

Listening for God: Prayer as Encounter

When we pray we are connecting with God. As in any other relationship, there needs to be time and space for listening - famously far more difficult than talking. Listening is often harder as we need to be attentive, holding back on our own thoughts and expressions, leaving space for the other person to fill. In this Chapter, we shall look at some of the ways in which we can be ready to hear God when He speaks in prayer.

We are sometimes suspicious or cynical over claims that God actually speaks to people today. In the TV series, *House,* the doctor says, "You talk to God, that's prayer; God talks to you, that's psychotic!" Yet many Christians claim that they have encountered God and heard Him. Have they *really* experienced sounds in the air? Some would say they have. Others would use the word "hear" figuratively, to denote an *inner* voice more felt than heard in the silence of their hearts.

Before considering ways in which God may speak to us, we need to distinguish carefully between "listening *for* God" and "listening *to* God." This is more than a matter of English grammar. As Christians, we can take the opportunity and make the space *for* God to meet and speak with us. This is not the same as being attentive when He actually does speak.

Preparing to Listen

So how do we listen *for* God? As with preparations for prayer more generally, Jesus's instructions to the disciples in Matthew 6 remain; we are to go into our room, shut the door, and pray in that secret place[53]. It may seem too obvious to point out, but should distracting thoughts arise it is useful for example to have a notebook nearby to jot down what comes in to our minds; in this way we can dismiss the thoughts (temporarily at least) and get back to our attentiveness. All these acts help to prepare the ground for God to encounter us; only this time, it is not what we will say, but what God will say, that forms the prayer.

The Old Testament story of the boy Samuel in the Temple[54] gives a practical example of the distinction between listening *for* God and listening *to* Him. In the story, one night when the formal worship of the day was over, Samuel was settling down to sleep when he heard a voice calling his name. Thinking it was the elderly priest Eli (Samuel was apprenticed to him), Samuel got up and ran over. Eli knew nothing about it and told Samuel to go and lie down. This happened three times. Eventually, after the third time Eli finally perceives that God was calling Samuel. This time Eli told him that should the voice call again, Samuel was to say, "Speak, Lord, for your servant is listening." [55] Eli was instructing Samuel to listen *for* God. Samuel did what he was asked. There was indeed a fourth call,

---

[53] Considered in Chapter Two.
[54] 1 Sam. 3:2-11
[55] 1 Sam. 3:9

Samuel was ready with his reply, and God spoke to him. The act of listening turned into an opportunity to listen *to* God.

How does God speak?

Bible reading is a crucial activity for followers of Jesus, and it is as we read that God may speak to us personally. But in order to hear Him, we need a listening space, somewhere God can meet with us and communicate with us directly. This *focused* listening arises from *deep* reading.

"Lectio Divina": Reading to Listen

Douglas Leonard in his book *Sacred Reading*[56] draws attention to a type of Bible reading called the "Lectio Divina" (Divine Reading). With this method, there is less emphasis on understanding the text (perhaps with the help of study notes or a commentary), and more on simply reading it without precondition. What happens is that the reader takes a passage of Scripture and reads through until a word or phrase 'jumps out' or clearly resonates with them, arresting their attention. At that point, the reader pauses and without going further dwells with the thought, going over the words again, following where the thought leads. In this act of following, it may well be that the reader will discover a fresh insight into an old truth, or perhaps a fresh relevance to their own situation. In short, the text will become vivid in a new way by revealing more of God and His purposes. God will have spoken.

---

[56] Douglas Leonard, *Sacred Reading*, (Notre Dame, Indiana: Ave Maria Press, 2017)

IMAGINATION MATTERS

It is not just through our intellectual capacities that God may speak to us. Truth can sometimes become apparent to us through a combination of imagination and feelings. St Ignatius Loyola, a sixteenth century Spanish saint, came to faith when, as a young fighter, he was recovering in a monastery from a wound he received on the battlefield. There were few books to read around him, except the famous 'Imitation of Christ' by Thomas a Kempis. Ignatius found that as he read about Jesus Christ his imagination was fired in an entirely unexpected way. Instead of dreaming about adding to his male prowess by winning daring fights he found himself imagining how it would be to undertake daring tasks for Jesus instead. He started to feel that God was close to him in an entirely new way, and this changed his life. Ignatius later taught the importance of imagination in Scripture reading as a way of opening the door to God to engage with us in a very personal and specific way[57].

Let's see how this approach may work in practice. Imagine for example the incident of Jesus and Jairus's daughter[58]. You will probably remember that embedded in this story is another healing miracle, where Jesus restores to health and fellowship a nameless woman who is identified simply by her medical condition ("an issue of blood"). Who amongst the characters in the story do you identify with? There is Jesus, the disciples, the crowd, and Jairus, anxious and distraught, begging Jesus to come and heal his seriously ill daughter. As Jesus is on His way, from behind comes someone else in need. How does it feel to see Jesus stopping and spending time with this unknown woman whilst Jairus's anxiety must be almost at breaking point? We might imagine Jairus's family. How would they be feeling? Very importantly, how does Jesus deal with this very

---

[57] See further John J. McGinty, *Spiritual Excercises of Saint Ignatius,* (New York: Doubleday, 1964)
[58] Mark 5:21-43

human situation? If we were standing there being a part of all this, how do we imagine He would deal with us? How would that feel?

This kind of imaginative exercise is not simply fanciful. Rather we are claiming a space for God to communicate with us based on Scripture, to speak with us, through our imagination and through what we feel.

The Holy Spirit Leads

How are we to understand what is happening when we read Scripture either using the "Lectio Divina" method or Ignatius' "spiritual exercise?" We have seen how the Holy Spirit is involved in maintaining our relationship with Jesus through prayer. It is that same Holy Spirit who inspired the Scripture writers and it is His continuing ministry to teach us about Jesus,

> When the Spirit of Truth comes He will guide you into all truth; for He will take what is Mine and declare it to you.[59]

So in reading Scripture in these thoughtful ways we are opening channels for the Holy Spirit to reach us and show us more about Jesus.

Many have powerful testimonies of the way in which God has met with them as they listen expectantly for His voice. Here are a few examples.

---

[59] John 16:13,14

John's[60] Story

John had a very short temper. Most of the time he could be calm, but it would not take much conflict before his heart pounded and - with his voice raised - a stream of ill-advised words and phrases would pour out, often hurting those around him. Always, afterwards, when calm returned, condemning thoughts rushed into his mind. He felt guilty, defeated, and ashamed. One day in prayer he felt prompted to read 1 Corinthians 1. As he was reading he got as far as verse 27, and then he stopped, unable to read further. His eyes filled with tears as he read,

> God chose what is low and despised in the world… to reduce to nothing things that are so that no one might boast in the presence of God. He is the source of your life in Christ Jesus.

John would say that he "heard" those words as if Someone were speaking to him. He felt Jesus Christ was reassuring his troubled mind with confirmation that he, John, was chosen by God, despite being "low" and "despised." Even more – John's whole life was derived from Jesus. He experienced an inner release and freedom from all the memories that condemned him, and he felt empowered to wrestle afresh with his destructive behaviour.

Notice how God used this Word uniquely to speak to John in his particular situation. Others reading that same verse on the same day may not have the experience John did.

Sandra's story

Sandra had recently retired early from a busy job as a senior manager and was looking forward to having more time to spend doing what

---

[60] The names have been changed in both John and Sandra's story.

she liked, not in a selfish way she would say, but having a bit more 'me time.' One morning she noticed some small bumps in her neck in the bathroom mirror. She had not given them much thought until one Sunday in church after the morning service she felt a conviction to seek medical advice. As the doctor was completing her examination of Sandra's neck, she discovered another, much larger lump, which up to that point Sandra had known nothing about. Suspecting cancer, the doctor arranged for tests and an urgent consultant appointment. Sandra felt as though the bottom floor in her life had been knocked out. As a Christian she was not afraid of death, but somehow now (suspecting the worst) it was the *process* of dying that filled her with sorrow and fear. Mostly it was the thought of saying so many 'good-byes' to those she loved, the children whom she would never see grow up. Sandra found that she was thinking about the story of Jesus and the raising of Lazarus, especially the words of Martha (and Mary later on),

> Lord, You had been here my brother would not have died.[61]

At some deep level, it really did feel to Sandra that Jesus was missing from her crisis. Yet as she turned to the chapter in her Bible, she found herself reading the part where Jesus says,

> This illness does not lead to death, rather it is for God's glory, so that the Son of God may be glorified through it.[62]

As she thought on these words, Sandra began to wonder whether the hope being offered was simply wishful thinking. So she prayed that God would give her a story out of her illness, a testimony she could bear to others and bring glory to God. Cancer was indeed confirmed and surgery followed. She sought healing ministry and knew the power of God sweep through her body as hands were laid on her in

---

[61] John 11:21
[62] John 11:4

prayer. Four years on, Sandra is free of the disease. She speaks of a new sense of closeness to Jesus; there is a gentle authenticity in her voice as she tells others of her healing. Sandra listened. God spoke.

As with John, God's message for Sandra was uniquely for her, the vividness of it speaking directly to her. As Douglas Leonard concludes,

> For the receptive soul, the Word of God has boundless power to illuminate and transform the prayerful believer.[63]

"Inward Fellowship"

Meditation is another way by means of which God may speak to us. Some Christians become anxious at the thought of meditation, as though its practice necessarily involves techniques borrowed from non (or pre-) Christian traditions. There is however, a strong Scriptural basis for meditation, and many faithful Christians down the ages have found great blessing through it.

So what *is* meditation? Essentially, it is "inward fellowship" with Jesus Christ. Richard Foster, writing in *Meditative Prayer*[64] quotes Thomas a Kempis' definition of meditation as growing into "a familiar friendship with Jesus." Foster goes on to describe what happens in meditative prayer, in particular that,

> We create the emotional and spiritual space which allows Christ to construct an inner sanctuary in the heart.[65]

---

[63] Leonard's work has been cited above.
[64] Richard J. Foster, *Meditative Prayer,* (Bromley: MARC Europe, 1985)
[65] Op. cit. p.9

He reminds us that the familiar picture of Jesus standing at the door and knocking, drawn from the book of Revelation[66] and immortalised in Holman Hunt's famous Victorian watercolour, was originally addressed to Christians. Jesus does indeed desire to be invited into our home and sit with us at the meal table, to be involved with our lives at this intimate level.

How do we welcome Him in? Foster describes three steps. Firstly, we are to "centre down," much in the same way as preparing for Divine Reading (as described above). This requires us to begin by noticing our thoughts, emotions, feelings, then gradually to let them go. In this sense it is the opposite state to restlessness and rush, distraction and agitation. God is with us, so we can let go. Secondly, Foster encourages us to "Behold the Lord." Here, a familiar verse or passage of Scripture, or maybe a picture that helps us visualise internally something of the wonder, majesty, glory, humility of God. In this condition of mind, we are ready for the third step, namely "the prayer of listening." It is impossible to anticipate what God may say to us then. It may well be for us as it was when the three disciples Peter, James, and John went up the mountain with Jesus, and He was transfigured before them.[67] Up on those hills, these disciples encountered God in a depth and vividness that took them quite literally to another place, way beyond what they could possibly have imagined. They were blessed with a meeting with Jesus in a magnificence they had never seen – they beheld His glory. Little wonder that this Gospel story ends by saying the disciples kept silent and told no one about what they had experienced. They probably had no words then to describe what they had seen and undergone: it was almost as if God had transported their perceptions to another level.

We have seen how individual prayer requires preparation; intentionally claiming the time and seeking the secret place where

---

[66] Rev.3:20

[67] Mark 9:2-8

we can meet Jesus and be fully open with Him. In that same secret place we listen for Him, waiting for His voice as we meditate on Him, using our feelings and imaginations as well as our minds as we read Scripture. In the next Chapter, we shall see how this rhythm of giving and receiving in prayer acts together to build up our relationship with God, and prepares the ground for something to take place that is truly transformational.

SUMMARY

All relationships need two-way communication, which is of course why listening is as important as speaking. Our relationship with God is no different, and individual prayer has a big part to play. Listening to God through a prayerful reading of Scripture is a way of tuning our spiritual ears to what God may be saying.

Listening has two parts: listening *for* God, and listening *to* Him. We are to create the space where we can listen *for* Him, and then pay attention as He speaks. We listen *to* Him as He holds us in the divine conversation.

There are many ways of doing this, but three methods in particular have stood the test of many centuries as Christians before us have been blessed in these ways. In each case, we ask God to help us hear what He wants to say.

❖ We read a Scripture passage carefully until a word or a phrase stands out and seems to command attention. Without reading on, we give thought and consideration mainly to

those words or phrase and wait on God (the 'Lectio Divina'-
divine reading - method)

❖ Pay attention to our feelings and imagination as we study
Scripture. This method was championed by St Ignatius
Loyola, a Spanish nobleman turned priest, in the sixteenth
century. He recommended making space for God to speak
to us in more than an intellectual way, through what we feel
and what we imagine.

❖ Meditation is another way of listening to God. This may
involve dwelling on a verse, or word, but might also include
an image or a picture, for example simply looking at the
Cross, and listen for God to speak to our hearts.

As and when He speaks, He does so to uplift, encourage, convict,
direct, or commission us. Let it not be lost; ensure it is written down,
to reflect on further or share with others.

REFLECTIONS

❖ Jesus has called us by name and given us the privilege of friendship with Him. How does it feel to be *involved* with Him in this way?

❖ How often are our individual prayers *simply* a rehearsal of our own 'agenda', (i.e. needs and concerns)? Might listening for God change this in any way?

PRAYER TOOLBOX – 4: LISTENING

Listening *for* God, creating the space, usually needs preparation.

✓ Try to find around 20 minutes to begin with.
✓ Look for some space where you are not likely to be interrupted for this time.
✓ To manage distractions, keep a pen and paper beside you to jot down on a 'to do' list anything you suddenly remember needs to be done, other than listening for God (you can pick this up at the end of your Listening time).
✓ It might also help to turn off your mobile phone…
✓ Pray those words of Samuel, "Speak, Lord, for Your servant is listening."

PRAYER TOOLBOX – 4: LISTENING (Continued)

Listening *to* God ("Lectio Divina" - Divine Reading):

- ✓ Ask the Holy Spirit to guide you, and wait quietly for a thought to come about where in the Bible you should start reading. If nothing comes, start with one of the Gospels.
- ✓ Read on until you find yourself paused over a word or phrase.
- ✓ Stop reading further at this point, and let your thoughts, feelings, and imagination dwell with the word or phrase.

Listening *to* God (Imagination as in the *Spiritual Excercises*)

- ✓ Take a story from the Gospels.
- ✓ Choose a character.
- ✓ Imagine the story from their perspective and ask yourself how would they feel, what would Jesus be saying to them?
- ✓ What may Jesus be saying to you through the story from this perspective?

Listening *to* God (Meditation):

- ✓ Read a verse, poem, hymn, worship song, or look at an uplifting picture as you seek to "Behold the Lord."

PRAYER TOOLBOX – 4: LISTENING (Continued)

At the end of your Listening time:

- ✓ Write down whatever you have heard (this can be used in your prayer time later on, and maybe reviewed some time later to see how God has used what He has told you).
- ✓ If anything worries you or makes you anxious after an 'Encounter' session, be sure to speak with a wise Christian friend. Remember the Bible was written *by* community *for* community and the Holy Spirit is present in His Church to help us understand and discover clearer meanings.

5

CONVERSATION WITH GOD: PRAYER AS TRANSFORMATIONAL

If we have been responding to God's invitation to meet Him through individual prayer, and have entered into the secret place intentionally to spend time with Jesus Christ, what happens next may surprise us. Why? Because we are involved with a *living* God who is active in His world. He inspires and encourages us as His friends to discover His ways and follow His paths. It is highly likely that we will experience change.

We may experience change at a number of different levels. To begin with, our ideas about individual prayer may change. As Sam Wells, an Anglican priest and author observes,

> The issue with conventional notions of individual prayer is that they used God rather than enjoy God. The intention is to get the outcome required; God is simply the best means of procuring it.[68]

---

[68] Samuel Wells, *Incarnational Ministry*, (London: Canterbury Press, 2017) 41

So, if we think God is simply a means to an end and individual prayer is mainly about trying to get Him to deliver, then prayer will become very one-sided and dull. We are likely to become disappointed - especially if nothing seems to happen as a result. The truth about prayer, of course, is very different, for God longs to connect with us and invites us to share with Him *in relationship* as we pray. As we have seen, this will entail listening to Him and seeking His will as well as sharing with Him our own needs and concerns. As Sam Wells concludes,

> Presence, attention, mystery, delight, participation, and partnership [are] all enfolded together. [Prayer is] a deeper experience of existence. It is the moment when disciples experience God's enjoyment of them.[69]

God *enjoying* us, delighting in us even though His work in us may not yet be complete. If this changes the way we think about God, then it may well be that our reticence to pray, or our expectations about what prayer will be like, will also change. The prospect of praying on our own may begin to feel like an adventure and not a chore, an exciting activity instead of perhaps a drudge.

Expect Personal Change

As well as changes to our ideas about prayer, we may also be faced with an invitation for *personal* change. We saw in the first Chapter how that the Holy Spirit is alongside us as we pray. He stays with us, He is within us. And He is in the business of change.

Scripture contains many stories of individuals being changed as they encounter God. We might remember for example Moses, who met

---

[69] Op. cit. p. 41

God at the burning bush[70]; Moses' life was never the same again. Or again, how about Zaccheus[71]? He changed his attitudes to money and wealth after he met Jesus. Instead of swindling people to get more money from them, Zaccheus wanted to give lots of it away. We think also of Nicodemus[72]. He was amazed to find out that Jesus – a Stranger - knew so much about him, and this recognition entirely changed his outlook. Think also of what happened to the woman at the well after she met Jesus and He asked her for a drink[73]. We can probably think of many more examples where, for so many, meeting Jesus changed their lives.

A Special Kind of Change

So what is special about the sort of change that meeting Jesus makes? Is it like the kind of change we achieve when giving our living room a makeover, or changing the colour of the front door because we could do with a fresh one? No, it is not a new covering over something old, not an add-on, not new wine into an old wineskin, but quite the opposite. The kind of change God brings about is *transformational* – a change that involves profound alteration, a remodelling, a reconstruction. We have just seen for example the evidence for Zaccheus's transformation was his changed attitude to money. This was no shallow make-over, no superficial alteration. What happened to Zaccheus was a root-and-branch conversion.

How did this happen? Perhaps part of the answer is that Jesus changed the way that Zaccheus saw himself. Because he was a tax collector for the Romans, everywhere he went he would have reminded the Israelites that they were a conquered people living

---

[70] Exodus 3:1-6
[71] Luke 19:1-10
[72] John 3:1-15
[73] John 4:29

under hated Roman authority. The hatred they felt for the Romans they would probably have shown to Zaccheus. Maybe he began to think of himself as some low-life who nobody wanted to know, worthless as a human being, despised and best ignored. Then Jesus passed by and looked for Zaccheus. We are not told how Jesus knew which tree to look at, or even how he knew about Zaccheus in the first place. We only know He wanted Zaccheus to be His friend (the offer of hospitality was a sacred duty in New Testament times and was taken as a gesture of friendship). In this way Jesus restored Zaccheus's self-respect, his sense of worth. He bathed in the warmth of Jesus's friendship, and those gifts from God came alive again in him. Zaccheus has only this small bit-part in the Gospel drama, and we never hear of him again. Was the change that came over him only temporary? Did he revert to his old ways once Jesus had left the place? We are not told. It is highly likely that he was never the same again, for God does not deal in half measures.

Our ideas about prayer, our views about ourselves (and how weak or inadequate we may think we are as disciples), our attitudes to others and to the world – in all of this God seeks to take us to new possibilities. He seeks to show us what might lie hidden beyond our horizons that have become cramped by memories of past failures. As He promised through Ezekiel, He will "put a new spirit within you."[74] As David Wilkinson writes,

> The invitation from God is to come into a transforming conversation with Him.[75]

In other words, amazingly yet simply, God begins the transformation process as we meet Him and hold conversation with Him in individual prayer.

---

[74] Ezekiel 36:26
[75] David Wilkinson *When I Pray, What does God do?*, (Oxford: Lion Hudson, 2015) 214

We are all very familiar with the idea of conversation. It is fundamental to how we *relate* to one another. We pay attention to each other; listen, as well as speak. In conversation, we learn about each other, we exchange ideas; our understanding deepens as we talk together. By means of conversation, we become friends. Through the conversation of individual prayer, we enjoy the amazing privilege of the friendship that God gives us. We speak to Him and listen for His voice in Scripture; we open up to Him in honesty and inward truth, and join in with His work through intercession. As Barbara Brown Taylor puts it in her book *The Preaching Life,*

> Mind and heart, spirit and flesh, are converted to a new way of experiencing and responding to the world...It is a matter of learning to see the world, each other, and ourselves as God sees us, and to live as if God's reality were the only one that mattered.[76]

In an amazingly miraculous but also mysterious way, when we pray we breathe the conversation of Heaven.

Appointed for Action

Jesus also told His earliest disciples that, as well as choosing them and calling them friends, He appointed them to go and "bear fruit."[77] In other words, Jesus does not expect His friends to be passengers, mere on-lookers at the party. Rather He has "set us aside," appointed us to be active, productive, out there in the world.

Of course, as soon as we become aware of His invitation and try to respond, we come across serious problems. For instance, we discover within ourselves that our desire to be part of His team is not always

---

[76] Barbara Brown Taylor, *The Preaching Life,* (Norwich: Canterbury Press, 2013) 44

[77] John 15:16

uppermost, not always our first priority. Sometimes life gets in the way, at other times our own motivations waver. There is always our unique catalogue of weakness, shortcomings, and wilfulness (that is, our own sin) to deal with. We really do come to God "rough-hewn", that is, our characters are like blocks of rough wood that need to be refined, purified, sharpened up, *transformed,* if the warping effects of sin are to be done away with. Then we can be more fruitful, to make a difference for God.

As we get to know Jesus through the conversation of individual prayer, we come to recognise that His will is so often about transformational change; transformations of situations, other people and, so importantly, ourselves. He changes our attitudes and perspectives. This in turn will energise us to bring about changes in situations that are truly transformational. Hidden potential becomes a reality.

We see evidence of this kind of change when we start to see Jesus in other people. In one famous Gospel passage, He taught that those who had been kind and considerate to the poor and disadvantaged had in truth been kind and generous to Him. The truth of this changed perception is brought out vividly in a legend about the English King Richard I, "the Lionheart." Having been out of the country for many years, he returned dressed in peasant's clothes, not wanting to draw attention to himself. Several nobles befriended him and were kind to him, unaware of his identity. One day, the 'peasant' accidentally tore his clothes and beneath the fraying cloth of his peasant's cloak, the friends saw the three red lions emblazoned on his tunic, and they knew him to be the king. What had been hidden was now clearly seen. The sight of the royal tunic made a deep truth clear to the nobles; while they had been kind to someone poor and otherwise insignificant, someone who could never hope to repay them, all along they had been dealing with the king himself, whose power and wealth lay far beyond theirs. When we start seeing

Jesus in the poor and the deprived, and that in serving *them* we are in truth serving *Him*, we are well positioned to make a difference and bring in more of God's Kingdom.

By way of illustration, I have chosen five examples below where Christians in their conversation with God recognised the kind of change He wanted. As they opened themselves to His transforming power, they went on to bring about the change they first saw as a possibility in the "transforming conversation" of individual prayer.

Phil's[78] Story

Phil was a widely respected worship leader in his fellowship. He loved his wife, but found relating to his in-laws extremely difficult. They were always kind to him, but he experienced constant tension whenever he was in their company. They frequently succeeded in "getting on his nerves." It occurred to him one day as he was in prayer, that of all the scores of individuals he prayed for, he did not actually pray for *them*. He was sure he had not intentionally *excluded* them, it was just that he had never got round to consciously *including* them. So he began to make them a part of his prayers. As he prayed for God to bless them he experienced what seemed to him like boulders and rocks in the way, blocking his imagination as to what "blessing them" might look like. Phil was troubled by this and begged God to show him what this blockage was about. Gradually over the course of the next few weeks, Phil began to recognise that he had not shown them how he valued them (if for no other reason than that they had brought his much-loved wife into the world and surrounded her with care). Eventually Phil came to the place where he could pray that he could move beyond his own selfishness and thus reach out to them in generosity and open-handedness. He

---

[78] Name changed to protect privacy.

61

found that the tensions when they were around all but disappeared and personal warmth took the place of his cold indifference.

The Holy Spirit graciously pointed out Phil's own shortcomings, the things he was putting into the mix that impaired his relationship with his in-laws. With this light, Phil altered his perspective and changed his behaviour. Grace, peace and blessing followed for all concerned.

Corrie's Story

Corrie Ten Boom was born in Haarlem, Netherlands; her family were devout and faithful. The Booms were members of the Dutch Reformed Church, and were very socially active, providing shelter and food for anyone in need. Corrie was fifty when the Nazis invaded the Low Countries in May 1940. The Boom's home became a refuge for Jews and other persecuted groups, and the family set up a small room where up to six people at a time could be hidden from the Gestapo. It is estimated around 800 Jews were saved. After a Dutch informant betrayed them, the Boom family were arrested; Corrie and her sister Bettsie were sent to Ravensbruck concentration camp. She and Bettsie suffered much hardship in the camp; Corrie said that she learnt much about prayer in the camp, especially that nothing was too small for God's love [79]. Bettsie died in December 1944, a few days before Corrie was released following a clerical error (shortly after her release all women of her age were executed). After the war, Corrie returned to Holland and created a rehabilitation centre for survivors of the camps, as well as Dutch nationals who had collaborated with the Germans during the occupation. Her ministry later became worldwide and she received many honours, including being knighted by the Queen of the Netherlands.

[79] Corrie Ten Boom *The Hiding Place,* (London: Hodder and Stoughton, 1971)

Forgiveness was probably her greatest witness. Sometime after the war ended, Corrie met the former German SS guard who had been particularly cruel to Bettsie at Ravensbruck. He was in a church where she had been speaking. All the old feelings of anger and vengeance swept through her when he came up to her.

> "How grateful I am for your message, Fraulein," he said. "To think that, as you say, He has washed my sins away!" His hand was thrust out to shake mine. And I, who had preached so often to the people in Bloemendaal the need to forgive, kept my hand at my side. "Lord Jesus," I prayed, "forgive me and help me to forgive him." I tried to smile; I struggled to raise my hand. I could not. I felt nothing, not the slightest spark of warmth or charity. And so again I breathed a silent prayer. Jesus, I prayed, I cannot forgive him. Give me Your forgiveness. As I took his hand the most incredible thing happened. From my shoulder along my arm and through my hand a current seemed to pass from me to him, while into my heart sprang a love When He tells us to love our enemies, He gives, along with the command, the love itself.[80]

Corrie's story shows the huge potential of a "transforming conversation" with God. As she discovered, He can work in the most severe circumstances as His friends look to Him through prayer and gain strength not only to carry on but also to transform lives around them.

Amy's Story

Seventeen-year-old Amy Carmichael was on her way home from church in a very fashionable part of Belfast one very wet day when she came across a poor old woman carrying a heavy bundle. Along with her two brothers, she took the bundle from the woman and

---

[80] Extract from *Prayer – Corrie Ten Boom* www.youtube.com/watch?v=4xAJA 1hNcUI

helped her along. As the "respectable" people around her pointed her out, Amy quickly realised she had unwittingly caused a minor scandal by associating with this poor woman. Amy recalled that just as they were going along,

> This mighty phrase flashed as it were through the grey drizzle: "Gold, silver, precious stones, wood, hay stubble — every man's work will be made manifest; and the fire shall try every man's work of what sort it is."[81]

The experience was so real that Amy turned to see who was speaking, but she saw nothing but a muddy street, and people with surprised looks on their faces. Amy recognised this as the voice of God.

That afternoon, Amy shut the door to her room and closed herself in with God. What happened that day would transform her by changing her priorities and her plans for life. She decided to turn her back on her life of wealth and privilege, and follow Jesus in His single-minded obedience to God. Amy began to reach out to the "shawlies" - girls who worked in the mills who were too poor to buy hats (considered the "proper" way to be in church), each girl covering her head instead with a shawl. Amy caused great offence to the other churchgoers when she brought the "shawly" girls. Her mother also came in for criticism for letting her daughter visit the slums to fetch them. Amy was not concerned; she knew these girls were very important to Jesus, and that she had a part to play. Jesus loved the "shawlies" through her, and they came to church in such large numbers that Amy needed a separate building for them. This was quite a challenge for Amy (then 22 years old), but she trusted God to provide. On 2 January 1889, "The Mill and Factory Girls' Branch of the YMCA" was opened. Amy- whose vision formed through her prayer had initiated the ministry and brought about the building - sat not on the platform but inconspicuously in the

---

[81] www.womenofchristianity.com

middle of the audience. Amy Carmichael firmly believed that God must increase, but she must decrease.

Later still, God called Amy to missionary work in India. While she was sad to leave her family, she did not hesitate. The same compassion God had inspired her to show to the "shawlies" this time focused on children, and here she met with a surprise. As a young girl she was disappointed with the colour of her eyes; instead of brown she wanted blue. She even prayed that God would change them and was very disappointed when it did not happen. Yet with her brown eyes, she was later permitted to go inside Hindu temples and rescue children destined for prostitution, thus changing their future. She spent the next fifty-three years in India setting up orphanages and ministering to the people she met.

Amy's story shows how God can transform outlooks and values through prayer. Amy was from a comfortable background, yet what she had learnt about Jesus – especially His kindness and compassion – led her to help the poor woman with her bundle. As Amy reflected on this meeting in her time of individual prayer, God led her to a series of life-changing decisions that resulted in her affecting the lives of countless people, giving them a hope for a future on earth and in heaven.

Bob's Story

In 1947 Dr Bob Pierce, an American evangelist and war correspondent, took a life-changing trip to China and Korea. He prayed a simple but powerful prayer, "Let my heart be broken by the things that break the heart of God." Amid the incredible poverty he encountered, he met one girl – "White Jade" - who represented the answer to his prayer. Bob gave her guardian five dollars (the last of his money) towards supporting the girl and maintaining her in school. He sent another five dollars every month, but wanted to do more.

In 1950, he set up the organisation World Vision to help children orphaned by the Korean War. Before long, World Vision supporters were sending money to care for children in need in other Asian countries, then in Latin America, Africa, Eastern Europe and the Middle East. Sponsors came from many new countries, including Britain; World Vision UK formed in 1982. From focusing on individual children, World Vision now works with whole communities in nearly 100 countries, following Jesus in working with the poor and oppressed to promote human transformation, seek justice, and bear witness to the good news of the Kingdom of God. The charity uses its global influence to ensure children are represented at every level of decision-making, becoming an influential voice on issues such as protecting children and child health. [82]

Bob Pierce's faith perspective was, like that of Corrie and Amy, formed through his prayerful encounter with God. Inspired by the transforming conversation of prayer, they have shared God's unconditional love.

Beatrice's Story

Beatrice Smith grew up in Rwanda where, as a child, prayer was an essential part of her life. She writes in her book *The Search for Home*[83] that prayer was one of the things she learnt most from her parents, confident that He would answer (and He always did). Beatrice's life changed completely when, in 1994 aged 10, she was caught up in the Rwandan genocide. Her home was attacked and together with her family she was forced to flee.

---

[82] www.worldvision.org.uk
[83] Beatrice Smith, *The Search for Home,* (Watford: Instant Apostle, 2016)

In her book, Beatrice tells many stories of God's provision for her and her family; I have selected just one. While their parents went out to try to find aid, Beatrice and her sister prayed for the whole day until it was dark. They grew hungrier by the minute. During the evening, a knock came at the door, and the girls were amazed to see a friend of their parents from Rwanda. He had heard about the family, particularly that they had been attacked and left for dead. He wanted to help. Seeing their plight, he provided food for the whole family and left an envelope for her father to open on his return. When the parents got back after a fruitless search, Beatrice gave her father the envelope left by the visitor. To their astonishment, it contained $200 – their money worries were over for at least six months.

Difficulties and challenges continued, until one night sleep proved impossible. Beatrice decided simply to pray, but could not even find the words. So,

> Instead I played a song, which in my mind captured everything I wished to say to God. I felt like I had lost a sense of who I was. I needed God to remind me, in the way that only He can. At three o'clock in the morning, something remarkable happened. My heart was spent in grief and I was still awake. With my eyes closed in surrender, I felt a breeze all around me and then a heavy presence of Jesus, as though He were standing right next to me. I felt hands that lifted me up and placed me on His lap and then began to comfort me. I felt comforting hands begin to stroke my hair as you would an upset child. I relaxed and let His peace wash over me as I sobbed over again. When I finally got my tears out, I heard a Voice say to me, 'I'm going to fix your broken wing, so you can soar again.' And with those words, I got up, went to bed, and haven't had a nightmare or anxiety attack since.'[84]

---

[84] Beatrice Smith, *The Search for Home,* (Watford: Instant Apostle, 2016) 165

There is much richness in Beatrice's story as she demonstrates not only that God answers prayer but also that He is to be found in places of darkness and uncertainty, wherever our "valley of the shadow" may happen to be.

Each person in these stories consciously sought Jesus's company in prayer. Through that "transforming conversation," they gradually acquired His outlook, and made His priorities their own. The result was that God's rule, God's kingdom, came nearer. Phil allowed more of God into his viewpoints and saw relationship problems resolve. Corrie was able to bless the prison guard who had been so harsh with her by handing over her own weakness in prayer and finding a strength not her own. Amy, Bob, and Beatrice found themselves caught up in God's transforming work as they rooted their relationship with Him in prayer.

Before closing this Chapter, there is one – sometimes unexpected - aspect of transformation I would like to explore.

Prayer as the Transforming Atmosphere

Psychologists tell us that the greater part of our mental lives is unconscious. Rather like the iceberg with 90% of its mass underwater, much of our inward motivation, choices, and behaviours arise from inward movements hidden from our conscious view. Similarly, the transforming effects of being in conversation with Jesus Christ through individual prayer may not be obvious to us.

There is a telling story from the Acts of the Apostles, where Peter and John had appeared before the court of the High Priest in Jerusalem. They had been spreading the good news about Jesus Christ – an activity strictly forbidden. Peter made a very challenging defence of his actions to the court. Those who heard them recognised that they had been with Jesus.[85]

Something about Peter and the way he spoke reminded them of Jesus. The text mentions boldness, and that the Apostles were uneducated and ordinary, but could it possibly be something more? Did these men (and later women, of course) carry with them some reflection of Jesus's manner, His bearing, His character even?

The early Apostles had kept company with Jesus and others noticed. We are familiar with the conscious copying (impersonating) of celebrities by some who want to dress or look like them. By contrast, maybe something about being with Jesus had "rubbed off" on the Apostles? They had absorbed something about Him simply by being with Him. Was this purely by what they said (or copied), or was it something less obvious but equally tangible? For example, when two people who know each other well spend a lot of time together sometimes they begin unintentionally to use each other's phrases and adopt their mannerisms. Maybe spending time with Jesus in individual prayer (the nearest we can get to His physical presence) can bring about a similar unconscious process, rather like a strong perfume lingers on the clothing long after the person wearing it has left the room.

This poem illustrates something of what I mean,

> Not only by the words you say,
> But in the most unconscious way
> Is Christ expressed.
> For me 'twas not the truth you taught,
> But when you came to me you brought
> A sense of Him[86]

---

85 Acts 4:13
86 Beatrice Clelland, *Indwelt*

When we are spending time with Jesus in prayer, our outlook and priorities will change. And although we all have feet of clay and struggle with more or less limitations, He will begin the transformation process with us, working in and through us, and more of His glory will shine.

SUMMARY

God is the Living One we meet through individual prayer. If we only think of prayer as trying to get God to do something our experience will be very limited – because God invites us in prayer to share in a "transforming conversation." He wants to change us, our outlook and priorities, so that they coincide with His own and He can use us more effectively to bring in His Kingdom; He will use us to transform a big or little part of the world around us. For example:

- God changed Phil's view of the difficulties he was having in personal relationships and transformed the family.
- God met with Corrie Ten Boom constantly through prayer in her time in Ravensbruck concentration camp, and transformed the desert of anger as she spoke with a former prison guard into streams of forgiveness.
- Through Amy Carmichael's encounter with a poor woman in genteel Belfast, God changed her priorities and later worked through her to transform the future for very many children in India.
- Bob Pierce sought God's heart through prayer and felt moved to do what he could for one child in poverty in Korea. The organisation he formed now works worldwide to minister in Jesus's Name to many thousands, transforming their lives and prospects.
- Beatrice Smith saw her life turn inside out during the Rwandan genocide. The habit of prayer she had learnt

from her parents became her own as she sought God's help during times of great need. She discovered the God Who transforms situations and people.

God can transform us with a reflection of Himself, even if we may not be aware of it.

REFLECTION

❖ Think about the description of individual prayer as a 'transforming conversation.' How far is this real in your experience?

❖ What strikes you about the people in the stories related in this chapter?

❖ Are you ready for the kind of transformational change God brings about?

PRAYER TOOLBOX 5

✓ Think of a situation that troubles you, personally, or in your community, your church, the world... Use your imagination to picture how God could bring about transformational change. Write it down. When you are in the "secret place" with Jesus, share it with Him regularly and wait for what happens.

6

WORKING WITH GOD: PRAYER AS PARTNERSHIP

One of the signs that our relationship with God in prayer is growing is that we come increasingly to share His priorities. In other words, what is important to Him becomes important to us. In this Chapter, we will look at intercession in prayer as way of working out those shared priorities. Working with God to get His Will done through intercession is a key expression of partnership with Him.

Alongside adoration and praise, it may well be that intercession is probably the form of prayer that Christians – from the earliest days - know best. In intercession, quite simply we are doing something on behalf of others, "bringing their needs to God." At its simplest, we are asking Him to do something with them, to them, or through them.

Sometimes people ask why this is important. For example, if God knows everything and knows what is needed, is not intercessory prayer telling Him what He already knows? What is the point in that? Why not just leave Him to get on with the task? Maybe we fail to see that we have an active part to play in moving God's purposes on. When we pray, "Your Kingdom come, Your Will be done," we are not meant to be submissive or passive (letting it all happen around us), but instead to know the joy of partnership with God in building His Kingdom.

When we turn the pages of the New Testament, it quickly becomes clear that earliest Christians "devoted themselves to prayer."[87] The early Church leaders were enthusiastic intercessors. We see from his letters that St Paul was regularly bringing before God the needs of the churches – and individuals - he knew well. For example, he told the Philippians that he joyfully thanked God every time he remembered them[88]; he told the Colossians he did not cease to pray for them[89], and that he constantly remembered the Thessalonian Christians when he prayed[90]. He reminded Philemon that he thanked God for him and his love.[91]

Intercession as Relationship-Building with God

When our prayer takes the form of intercession, we have the opportunity to *know* Jesus better, as distinct from simply knowing *about* Him. In so doing, He draws us into a closer relationship with Himself.

This seems quite a claim. To think of friendship on a human level, one of the joys friends soon discover is that someone else thinks or believes *like them;* the natural distance between them collapses, and isolation melts into the intimacy of shared thoughts, a shared outlook on life, perhaps even shared passions. A deeply authentic example of this occurs in an episode of the BBC TV comedy series

---

[87] Acts 2:42

[88] Phil. 1:3,4

[89] Col. 1:9

[90] 1 Thess. 1 2,3

[91] Philemon 4

The Vicar of Dibley, a very unlikely place perhaps. During her first sermon, Geraldine Grainger (the new vicar) describes being called to the Ministry after she felt "blown away" when reading Jesus's Sermon on the Mount for the first time; His words deeply resonated in her heart. So when it comes to friendship with Jesus, we can discover the joy of finding everything we have in common with Him, His outlook, His passions. Perhaps this what Jesus meant when He said to His disciples that they were His friends, because He had shared with them everything He had learnt from His Father.[92] We use several of phrases to describe this sense of unanimity, such as "being on the same page" as someone, or "being on the same bus." Intercession is a way of praying "on the same page" as Jesus, as His outlook becomes increasingly our own. We saw for example in the last Chapter how Bob Pierce prayed, "Let my heart be broken by the things that break the heart of God." In this way, Bob drew very close to the heart of God as he prayed *according to God's Will.* So when our hearts burn with a sense of injustice when we hear about how women and children are trafficked, or when the poor are oppressed and immigrants are discriminated against, and pray that God will move to change the situations, we know we are on the "same page" as Jesus.[93]

Receiving His Gifts - Eternally

Getting to know Jesus through intercession also gives us the opportunity to share in two of His very precious gifts. He spoke about '*My* joy'[94] and '*My* peace'[95], gifts that belong to Him and arise only from being in relationship with Him, a precious connection that death does not break. It is quite amazing to imagine that Jesus

---

[92] John 15:15
[93] See for example, Isaiah 58:6-7
[94] John 15:11
[95] John 14:27

calls us friends in the first place, and even more so that He wants us to share His joy and peace as we partner with Him in His work through intercession.

Being "There" for Jesus

Two more of Jesus's sayings seem to point towards the truth that knowing Him, especially through sharing His concerns and passions, will also have eternal consequences. Firstly, when He is cautioning about false prophets (those who will burst on to the world stage claiming to be His special mouthpiece, but whose lives do not match up), He warns that not everyone who pays Him due respect (by calling Him "Lord") will enter the kingdom of Heaven.[96] It is evident from what follows that many of these false prophets enjoyed very successful and spectacular ministries. For example, they complain that they prophesied in His Name, cast out demons and performed many miracles, yet Jesus tells them that He never *knew* them. Amazingly - given their apparent "success" – it turns out that their preoccupations were never *His;* they were perhaps more concerned with the coming of their own kingdom and expanding their own success than they were about His.

Secondly, on another occasion, Jesus told His listeners that anyone who acknowledged Him in this life, He would acknowledge them before His Father in the next.[97] Behind the Greek word - *homologein* - translated "acknowledge" lies the idea of sameness from which we get the English word "homologous," an adjective used to describe two things that have a close similarity or function. At the very least then, Jesus seems to be saying that if our concerns are similar at root to His, and we live (and pray) out of that experience, then we will be part of *His* concern not only in this life but also when we stand

---

[96] Matthew 7:21-23
[97] Matthew 10:32

at Heaven's gate. To put this very crudely (but hopefully without too much distortion), there seems to be the suggestion that if we are there for Him in this life, He will be there for us in the next as well as this.

Intercession as Partnership between Friends

In Scripture, our attention is drawn continually to the fact that God chooses to use ordinary human beings to bring about His purposes. There are so many examples. We can think of Moses perhaps, whom God commissioned to lead the Israelites out of slavery in Egypt to the freedom of the Promised Land. Many of the Prophets of the Old Testament experienced a commissioning, that is, being called, set apart and empowered to deliver God's Message to His people. Women too had a partnership role to play. As part of His great plan of redemption and restoration, God chose to become a human being through a process of birth. For this, God chose Mary. Through her agreement and willingness, God the Son entered His world.

The amazing privilege that is ours as Christians is that in calling us His friends God asks us to partner with Him to work His purposes through us and with us. He wants *His* concerns and passions to be *ours* as well. We are not to be passive onlookers, but fully aligned to God's purposes, using our gifts and energies, fully embracing the huge privilege of being His fellow-workers.

Fellow-Workers with God through Intercession

When we begin to recognise that God seeks to use us to build His Kingdom on earth by extending His Rule here, we are close to the heart of understanding intercessory prayer. But we know that the world is teeming with need, there are countless places where God's

Kingdom needs to come, so the question is, "Where do we start?", "Who do we intercede for?", "How do we intercede?"

Old hands at intercession know of at least two key and opposite dangers. One stems from our (accurate) perception of the myriad needs in our world, like famine and war, which tragically affect so many. The danger is that if our intercessions are much generalised we may not be able to identify any part we may can play, any specific need to focus our intercessions on. We may also miss sharing God's joy when there are positive outcomes in the situations we are praying for. As I write, there is much rejoicing that a Christian Pakistani woman, Asia Bibi, who had been awaiting the death sentence since 2010 for alleged blasphemy, has had her case dismissed. Many Christians have been faithfully praying for her through this time and are thanking God for the courage of Pakistan's Supreme Court and for Asia regaining her freedom. While news of her release is an occasion of great thanksgiving, loyal intercessors have a renewed focus for prayer, namely that she will be able to enjoy her freedom in her home country. Again, Nigeria recently embarked on a General Election. It was greatly feared that the long queues waiting to cast their vote would become a target for terrorist attack. Groups of Christians around the world prayed. It happened that not only was this the most peaceful election for many years, but that the handover of power by the outgoing President (Goodluck Jonathan, himself a Christian) was without rancour or delay. Through specific focuses for intercession as in these examples, and seeing change in those situations, it very much looks like that God gives us a little part in extending His Kingdom of peace and justice in the world.

The other danger arises from the same perception: "There is so much need out there, shall we just keep our prayers local?" The problem arises when our intercessions become so localised and "parochial" (in the unhelpful sense) that we forget God's concern for His *world* and His desire to partner with us to achieve His Purposes in all of it.

BALANCED INTERCESSIONS

Thinking about avoiding these two dangers, Timothy received some wise advice from St Paul about the importance of praying for "kings... and everyone in high positions,"[98] while James urged prayers for all who are sick[99]. These recommendations from early Church leaders help us become aware of the need for balance in the matters we bring to God in intercession - between local and global, near at hand and far away. But is there anything else that might help?

Where to Start?

The Ephesian Christians were told that,

> We are what He has made us, created in Christ Jesus for good works which God prepared beforehand to be our way of life.[100]

Thus, we are part of God's provision for His world in our own place. We have a particular role, a ministry to live out, unique to our time and unique to *us* as individuals. Who we are, our natural gifts, abilities and interests, have a divine origin. Of course, we know that some of this natural equipment may need refining and re-calibrating in the light of God's Kingdom. We also know well that one person does not weight the same issues, the same concerns, in the same way as someone else. For example, some are very committed to God's care for His Creation and are ardent about climate change and its impact on the poor; others are more passionate about world peace. Many others long to see the Gospel spreading. These matters of course overlap, as they are all features of God's Kingdom. Looking again at Jesus's instructions about prayer in Matthew 6 (in particular

---

[98] 1 Tim. 2:1-3
[99] James 5:14-16
[100] Ephesians 2:10

that we are to go into our *own* room to pray)[101] we can see that He wants us to pray with the passion and commitment that arises from how He has made us. We intercede from that place with the freedom, patience, and persistence.

We can ask ourselves therefore, "Where do we want God to act? Where do we long to see God's Kingdom come?" We could start our intercessions from there.

Like other aspects of individual prayer, intercession is intensely practical, so we shall now consider some hands-on suggestions for developing realistic intercessory prayer.

Pray Specifically (Not Just "God Bless…")

I remember some Christians being astonished when a new believer came up to them after church one morning and, instead of asking, "How are you?" said, "Have you been blessed this week?" Seeing their hesitation, she explained that they had been on her prayer list that past week and she had prayed that they would be blessed; she simply wondered what might have happened.

Jesus had a passion that people would come to Him and receive Him and His wonderful gifts. It is sometimes challenging to ask Christians whether they are praying for individuals they know, by name, that they come to a saving knowledge of Jesus. Jesus too intercedes for His Disciples, for example once said to Peter that He was praying for him "that his faith did not fail."[102]

---

[101] Considered in Chapter Two.

[102] Luke 22: 32

KEEP A PRAYER LIST (AND KEEP IT UP TO DATE)

Even with the popularity of on-line shopping, many still maintain a list to help them remember what they need to buy. If people still send them, how many fewer Christmas cards would be sent if people did not maintain a list? We keep lists to help us remember or, to put it another way, to stop us forgetting.

It may seem obvious (or even irreverent), but it can be the same with our intercessions. If we are praying specifically, it makes sense to remember who and what we are praying for. It may be easy to remember what is uppermost in our minds at any one time, but also easy to forget people or places where God's Kingdom can come. Most churches and many missionary associations publish prayer diaries to help focus prayer. We can and should use these but also develop our own, not only to help us remember, but also gives us space to record answers to prayer as and when they arise. I know of Christians who keep a prayer notebook in this way, and one in particular who has written on the front cover some words from Jeremiah,

> Call to me and I will answer you, and will tell you great and hidden things that you have not known.[103]

The prayer list can so often become a book of blessings as prayers answered become a basis for praise.

PRAY EXPECTANTLY (THAT GOD WILL DO SOMETHING / SOMETHING WILL HAPPEN)

There is often a wry smile when Christians read in the book of Acts about St Peter's miraculous release from prison[104]. The story described

---

[103] Jeremiah 33: 3
[104] Acts 12: 5-16

how many of the faithful had gathered for prayer (doubtless for Peter's release), yet when Rhoda the servant girl answered the frantic knocking on the door and found Peter himself standing there and ran to tell the gathering, no one believed her. So much prayer, yet so little expectation that anything would happen. I guess many of us on occasions would be on common ground with these early Christians.

Some of this lack of expectation may stem from a respect for what we conceive as "God's Will" and not to appear "pushy" with God (if such a thing were possible). But the upshot may well be that we do not pray with the passion of those who *cry* to God. Instead, our assumed deference to His Will turns into a sneaking belief that God is not interested in our prayers. Worse, we may feel that if we are too expectant in our prayers we run the risk that we are attempting to get God to do what *we* want, instead of what He wills.

We know that He wants us to partner with Him in taking forward His Kingdom and His will. Prayers of intercession are a key part of this commission. So when we are praying according to His will is it not entirely legitimate to be whole-heartedly expectant that He will respond, out of His graciousness? Expectancy like this could be described as faith. We see an example of this in Jesus's ministry. On one occasion Jesus asked someone who came to Him for help whether they believed He could do what they asked [105]. We read that in Nazareth, for example, He could achieve little because there was so little faith[106]. Do we believe that God is living and real, and that He will hear and answer prayer? Do we fully grasp that He has a Will, and has made promises He intends to keep?

---

[105] Matthew 9:28
[106] Mark 6:5,6

God is not human, that he should lie, or a mortal, that he should change his mind. Has he promised, and will he not do it? Has he spoken, and will he not fulfil it?[107]

We are allowed to be bold and expectant.

PRAY PERSISTENTLY

A common reason Christians give for praying intermittently (or not at all) is that nothing seemed to happen when they did pray. For example, some gave up their faith altogether when, despite much prayer, a deeply loved person was sick and did not recover. Others, looking out into the world, conclude that praying achieves little if anything to change the warfare, famine, or suffering.

When Jesus talked *about* prayer, He said His followers would need to be persistent. In fact, Luke tells us in an editorial note that Jesus told a parable directly related to the situation of apparently unanswered prayer – the one that we know as the Parable of the Unjust Judge. In particular, that it was important "to pray always and not lose heart." [108] Jesus even suggests that answers to prayer may seem so long delayed that believers will still be praying for an answer when He comes again in glory. Jesus knew that answers would sometimes not be apparently forthcoming for those who pray. Through this parable, He teaches us that (a) our prayers are heard and (b) God will act. Sometimes we need the gift of perseverance not to give up when it seems too hard to hold onto these two truths.

The other key point is that God's response to our prayers, no matter how heart-felt or sincere, may not be what we would expect or perhaps would want. Jesus Himself had this experience in Gethsemane's

---

[107] Numbers 23:19
[108] Luke 18:1-8

garden[109]. There we see Him in the intensity of deep prayer, pleading with His Father that the cup of His suffering would pass. Yet it does not, and Jesus – the wrestling over – stands to wait for the betrayer and willingly accepts the path that leads to the Cross. St Paul wrote about a "thorn in the flesh." It is not known exactly what this was, but it was enough to make him pray three times that God would take it away. Instead of doing so, St Paul received an assurance that God's grace was all-sufficient, and His strength would be discovered in weakness.[110]

So even if nothing seems to happen when we pray, God still hears and will draw our prayers into a fresh willingness to serve Him. Even when nothing seems to be happening, we may remember St James words, "The prayer of the righteous ... is powerful and effective." [111]

The film *The Heroes of Telemark* is a wartime story of courage and heroism, following a group of Allied commandos sent to Norway to disable a chemical facility being used by Nazi scientists to develop Hitler's nuclear bomb. As part of the plan, two of the commandos set out to destroy a huge dam used to generate power for the factory. They lay their explosives deep inside the dam and quickly make their getaway to a place of concealment before detonating their bomb. There is a muffled, small explosion, then – nothing. The expressions on the faces of the commandos are a study: the jubilation of one gradually drains away as panic takes hold seeing that the massive dam – despite their efforts - is still intact. The other, a demolition expert, calmly reclines in their hiding place, placidly tamping his pipe, encouraging his mate to be patient. Later – much later – the two commandos, the one anxiously surveying the dam through binoculars, the other still peacefully expectant, see first a tiny crack appear followed by a small spurt of water, then gradually another,

---

[109] Matthew 26:39
[110] 2 Cor. 12:9
[111] James 5:16

then another, until a big concrete chunk of dam wall breaks and a colossal torrent of water sweeps away what is left. The dam is in ruins.

Archbishop William Temple once said that when he prayed, he saw coincidences happen, and when he stopped praying, there were no longer any coincidences. It may be that the effectiveness of our prayers remains unseen, and we may not know how God has used them until He shows us in Eternity.

SUMMARY

We have looked at several facets of our relationship with God which are opened up and fed by individual prayer, namely:

- Being open with Him in an atmosphere of honesty,
- Receiving from Him whatever He has for us as we listen,
- Bring transformed through the conversation of prayer.

There is a fourth facet - partnering with Him to bring about His Kingdom through intercession, something we pray for every time we say "Your Kingdom come" in the Lord's Prayer.

In intercession, we are quite simply asking God to do something with others, to them or through them. We pray for the world, the people, the issues, the concerns that (from our practice of listening to Him) we know matter to Him. When those same things matter to us, when what breaks His heart breaks ours too, and we feel the extent to which He carries our burdens and pains, we are beginning to experience the character of the friendship with God that Jesus conferred upon His followers.

As with all aspects of relationship, we need a certain degree of discipline (that is, regulation, and order) if our intercession is to be effectively focused. For example, to pray specifically for someone and their needs (or a nation, or wider concern), as distinct from simply "God bless" creates a focus for an expectation that God's Kingdom will come in that place *at that point*. He calls us to labour together with Him, praying with passion, and patience.

As we intercede, are we expectant that God will do something in response? Archbishop William Temple famously remarked on one occasion that we he prayed, coincidences happened, but when he did not pray, there were no coincidences either.

The importance of persistence, of not giving up, is crucial. It is well beyond our present knowledge of the God Who calls us into relationship to understand why there are delays in prayers being answered, but the attitude of not giving up was important enough for Jesus to tell a parable about it (Luke 18:1-8). Persistence therefore takes its place alongside passion and patience as three vital elements within prayers of intercession.

REFLECTION

❖ Do we really believe that prayer changes anything?

❖ Have we ever given up praying because nothing seems to change? What may help us to carry on with persistence?

❖ Individual prayer as intercession can be hard work. Are we ready for our hearts to be broken with what breaks God's?

PRAYER TOOLBOX – 6: PARTNERING WITH GOD – INTERCESSION

✓ Spend a little time recognising where *you* want God's Kingdom to come – people, places, nations, issues… Where do your passions and His meet? Start interceding from here.

✓ Build and use a prayer list (and keep it up to date).

✓ Pray specifically (not just "God Bless.")

✓ Pray expectantly that God will do something / something will happen.

✓ Pray persistently.

7

Connected with God: Prayer as Personal Culture

Before Facebook, Instagram, Twitter and so many other social media platforms provided ways for people to keep in touch, the website Friends Reunited was very popular. It appealed to all who were looking to get back in touch with old friends from schooldays, college, previous jobs, or new friends perhaps once met on holiday. By the time it closed in 2016, many had been able to link up again and re-kindle old friendships, helped by the lists and message boards on the site.

The initial popularity of Friends Reunited illustrates a very important point about friendships. Despite the best of intentions, life happens and sometimes friendships start to drift, and unless friends make the effort to keep in touch, relationships can be lost. We know that relationships flourish if we invest in them – our time, thoughts, energy, but also that they begin to wither if we start to ignore them. Sometimes they can die altogether through neglect. Sadly, what can be true of lost friendships also applies to lost relationships within a family.

In the previous Chapters, we have been exploring how our relationship with God can grow and develop through the connection of individual prayer. There is a clear link between what happens within our prayer life and the vitality of our relationship with God. It also seems to be the case that if we start to ignore our prayer life, the opposite begins to happen - we are at risk of drifting off into a sleep of carelessness about God. We considered the Holy Spirit's ministry of the wake-up call in Chapter One, but we also have a responsibility to keep our prayer activities alive, and this will involve a habit, a daily pursuit. As the writer of 2 Chronicles advised, "Turn to the Lord, your strength, seek His Presence always."[112]

Investing in the Relationship

Our individual prayer activities are well embedded in our lifestyle if we are maintaining our friendship with God. Giving a priority to our prayer life, regularly sharing with God, listening to Him and being available to partner with Him in Kingdom-building means not missing prayer out when life gets in the way.

While not all Christians aspire to be elite athletes, even maintaining basic levels of health and well-being requires some form of regular exercise. Our spiritual fitness is similar. If we are to remain vitally connected with God in relationship then our prayer time is to be embedded in our daily routine, integral to our lives, at the heart of what it means to be "us."

Our Choices Make Us Who We Are

We sometimes use the phrase "a way of life," or "lifestyle" to describe someone's habitual choices about the way they spend their time or

---

[112] 1 Chron. 16:11

their money, and what interests they pursue. It is quite remarkable that, even though human beings can be so famously inconsistent, it is still possible to identify behaviours that are customary, the things that seem to give us an identity as individuals. My lifestyle, like yours, is the result of accumulated choices, some free, others imposed, and helps give me my identity; it helps to describe who I am.

Prayer As Part Of Our Personal Culture

For Christians, our relationship with God makes us who we are. We have an identity in Him, full of huge privileges and blessings. For example, He knows us by name, calls us into His service, and creates an enduring relationship that even death cannot destroy - and this is only the start. God draws us into a culture of connection and links us into a friendship with Him through individual prayer.

Maintaining this link is part of how we live. Our lifestyle is drawn around our prayer life, which becomes the foundational framework of our personal culture. Embedded in our daily schedule, praying is the regular activity, the backbone to all the other parts of our lives. It is the savour that flavours our whole way of being.

How Do We (Re)kindle Our Desire to Pray?

Some of us miss out on this huge and almost unimaginable offer of friendship with the Living God through prayer (which we may not yet have started, or perhaps even given up).

The key thing is of course that we *want* the fellowship with God that prayer makes possible. In Chapter One I compared the sensation of smelling delicious food being prepared with catching a fresh glimpse of the joy of friendship with God. The aroma of the food may remind us how hungry we are; we savour the flavours and eat to become satisfied. Similarly, the God who longs to bless may create in us a longing for Him like a spiritual thirst, dazzle us with a sign of His Presence, or simply prompt us deep in our consciousness. He is the God who delights in us, not the false god who lays guilt-trips. He seeks to remind us that He is on our side, wanting to welcome us "at His party," and longs to bless us through the connection of prayer.

The question for each of us is simple: do we want a closer relationship with the living God? Do we want our connection with Him to grow? If the answer to that question is "yes," then God may be taking us to a new place, somewhere to make a new start, through the practical step of regular prayer.

Building the Prayer Habit

To keep our relationship with Him vital, energising, dynamic and firm we need a rhythm in our prayer life – a rhythm energised by habit. Our challenge is to maintain a prayer life that will nourish that inner relationship with Him, so that we can become rooted and grounded in Him, realising the life of the Vine in us His branches.

Many of us know more about what it takes to break a habit than to make one, but whether we are breaking or (as in this case) making a new habit, nothing will happen until we make a decision; our decision is where all habit-related matters begin. Having taken the step and decided to build a prayer habit, a lot of advice and guidance about habit-building more generally is equally useful. I have summarised below the seven steps that are common to many habit-building schemes.

Keep It Simple

Do not attempt too much too soon. Better a five-minute period that you want to add to than a twenty-five minute period that is too much to keep up. It will also be important to plan closely what your prayer will consist of. It may follow the same format each day or be varied across a pattern of a few days. Perhaps you will decide to use a set format to help you (there are many websites with daily prayer suggestions), such as the Church of England's *Daily Prayer*[113].

Plan the Time

What time for prayer works best with your timetable? Do you have more time at weekends than on weekdays? Work out how much time you want to spend in prayer then plan your start date. There is a balance to be struck between being too rigid (for example, "I always pray at nine o'clock precisely") as this could be too easily disturbed, and its opposite, which would be having no time of the day set aside. It will always be preferable to choose a five-minute period twice a day and keep it up than to decide on a different plan that may be too much of a stretch. Choosing a time period when you expect the daily routine to be reasonably stable will also help your new prayer habit to bed in.

Decide Your Trigger

Setting up a new habit clearly requires a change to take place in the daily routine, so a prompt to remind you of the time set aside for prayer may be necessary. Everyone has a different "reminding strategy" – some may put a sticker on the kitchen door or write a note in their diary. The key thing is to recognise that the prayer habit

---

[113] www.churchofengland.org/prayer-and-worship/join-us-in-daily-prayer

needs a prompt each day for it to form, and take a step to plan how this may work for you.

KNOW THE PROCESS

Psychologists tell us that our brains are wired in such a way that it takes anything from twenty-one to thirty days to acquire a habit, but repetition is the key. It may seem strange at first to be praying regularly (as with any other activity we want to become habitual), but this is likely to pass as the recurrence becomes more established. There may be pitfalls on the way. On one particular day, we may not feel like it, or something unexpectedly crops up that disturbs the developing routine. This is all entirely natural and does not mean anything is going wrong. Remember that you are trying to make an important change to your lifestyle, and the process of adapting to the new routine is not always straightforward. It is important not to try developing all sorts of revisions to the plan during the initial process; if the new routine does not seem to be bedding in, have courage and start again. You can review everything that has taken place at the end of your habit-forming period when (say twenty-one to thirty days), and make any changes or improvements then. Knowing the process will guard you against getting discouraged and considering giving up.

KEEP YOUR EYE ON THE GOAL

We have seen how God the Holy Spirit is the Motivator for those who want to start, renew or refresh their prayer lives, and there is a process to be gone through as with every other habit formation. For example, those who tip out of bed at an early hour to spend time in the swimming baths because they are in training for a swimming gala do so because they have their eye on the medal, or improving their own personal best. People on a fat-reducing diet who turn down the offer of a cream cake do so because they want to acquire the benefits that weight loss will bring. Likewise, Christians need to be so clear about the benefits that a renewed prayer life will bring that it has the power to keep them going. This is where a decision to pray based simply on an idea of obligation is likely to come unstuck (except perhaps for the most self-disciplined amongst us). We looked in the Introduction to this book how important it is that a fresh vision of God energises us as we come to pray, in the same way as an aroma of delicious food may stimulate our appetites, or our eyes are lit up by the dazzling colour of a diamond refracting natural light. This fresh vision (be it brand new or an old one somehow re-gilded) is especially important in building the prayer habit, as it will be *this* vision that sustains us as we progress. Wanting more of what God wants for us is often reason enough for building and maintaining a regular prayer life, but identifying the reason why *you* want to pray (or start praying again) is crucial. It may be a good idea to write out "I want to pray today because." – And you fill in the gap and adopt this as your goal. God will bless you as you pray, and you will discover new ways in which He Himself is your reward.

Choose a Running Partner

The Church – "God's wonderful idea" – is the faith community to which all baptised Christians belong. We were never meant to go-it-alone in our discipleship, so our Christian friends are the "go-to" place for encouragement and support. We will benefit from their companionship as we look to deepen our relationship with God by renewing our prayer lives, just as those setting out to raise their physical fitness through running report how valuable it is to run with a partner. God Himself is of course the Supreme Encourager, and He draws others into this ministry. It may be that someone from your fellowship will agree to, as it were, walk beside you in the habit-forming period and commit to pray for you as you embark on this new adventure. At the very least, share your plan with your Church leader.

REVIEW AND EXPERIMENT

It will probably be a good idea at the end of the habit-formation period (around three to four weeks after the start date) to sit down with your running partner and review with them what has gone well. For example, basic things like "Was the time I chose the best one?" or "How many days did I manage?" Out of this review process, you may decide on changes, such as time or place.

The whole Church is called to prayer, but because we are all different, some aspects of prayer will be more congenial to some than to others. As part of the review it will be useful to be clear about those aspects of prayer that you have discovered to be very meaningful *and* plan to develop those other aspects that may take you out of your comfort zone. For example, some find being quiet with God much harder than coming before Him with a list of many names and concerns. Perhaps God the Holy Spirit wants to draw you to explore these less congenial aspects of prayer as well so that He can bless you and better equip you for His Kingdom-work.

It will be especially important to recognise where God has blessed you in this period. Perhaps the dynamic of His relationship with you may have given you a renewed assurance of His love, and fresh insights into His purposes. If any changes to the format of your developing habit are necessary, work them in to your routine and go again.

Living in fellowship with God, "abiding in the Vine," is of course not principally about techniques; above all else it is about relationship with Him. But for the relationship to grow, the foundation of ordered, habitual prayer is crucial part of personal culture. This is the pathway to greater awareness of God in Jesus Christ, and leads to a broader availability for His Kingdom-building service.

SUMMARY

We can respond to God's invitation to relationship through individual prayer. Yet a relationship is not a static thing; it is either going forwards or backwards. Prayer helps to maintain our relationship with God and move it forward, to keep our connection with Him full of life. But this does not happen by accident. To make prayer a part of our personal culture, part of "who we are," means building a prayer habit we can keep.

PRAYER TOOLBOX – 7: BUILDING THE PRAYER HABIT

✓ Make the decision to start – nothing starts without a decision.

✓ Keep it simple – try to avoid being too ambitious at the beginning.

✓ Plan the time - when will you begin the habit-forming period, how long, when (and where) you will spend the time each day? Plan the content of your prayer time, too.

✓ Decide your trigger – what will remind you to pray?

✓ Know the process – habit-forming involves personal change, and this can sometimes produce difficulties.

✓ Keep your eye on the goal – be able to complete the statement, "I want to pray today because I -" in a way that will fire your desire to achieve.

✓ Choose a "running partner" – God does not expect His disciples to be alone on the journey.

✓ Review and Experiment – take note with your running partner of what has gone well, and how God has blessed you. If life has got in the way, make any necessary changes and run again. You can never make too many new starts!

Conclusion

Record numbers of people in the UK and US would say that they have no religion, yet over half of all adults in the UK pray, reported *The Observer* newspaper recently.[114] There is a similar proportion in the US. Half of that number thought that God heard them when they prayed. If you went into the street in your nearest town with a sketchpad, stopped a random bunch of ten adults, and asked, "Could you draw a picture of prayer?" I wonder what their pictures would look like.

Some might draw a pointed mountain with the word "God" somewhere beyond the top, and a group of little dots at the bottom representing people who pray. If you asked them to explain a little, they might tell you that God is "out there" and prayer somehow bridges the gap.

Is God somehow "out there," not moving from the top of His mountain? Are we "down here," trying to find a way up to Him? Is prayer the action that somehow bridges the gap between us? The truth could not be more different. Our Christian faith does indeed reveal the God who is "out there," but importantly He is a God who is not content to *stay* there whilst human beings try to find a way to Him. Probably above all else, He shows Himself to be *the loving God who goes out looking*. Scripture tells how God began His search

---

[114] *The Observer*, Sunday 14 January 2018

for friendship and fellowship with the human race. It began with Creation[115], then through the call of Abram to the subsequent story of the Jewish people. Ultimately God extended His invitation to embrace the whole world through Jesus [116]. He leaves His home and comes searching. This is deep mystery hard to grasp[117], but when Jesus – God the Son – born of Mary came to earth, this was indeed "*God* with us."

Jesus spoke often about seeking and searching. On one occasion, He said plainly that He had come to seek and to save those who were lost[118]. At other times, He used pictures to speak the same truth. He told the story of the shepherd who lost one of his sheep and went out to look for it[119]. He told another about a woman who lost a coin and searched high and low until she found it. And who can forget the story of the Prodigal Son - he was "lost" and on his return, was "found." In each of these stories, the shepherd, the woman at home and the father of the Prodigal are all equally joyful when they find what (or who) they are seeking. Their search ends in a joyous re-uniting with what had been lost. In these pictures, Jesus of course is showing us the longing heart of God.

When He has found us, there is indeed a "new creation,"[120] similar to being born for a second time[121]. No matter in what way we may

---

[115] This seems to me to be a truth whether or not the account of human origins in Genesis 2 and 3 is a literal account of what happened. My point is that human beings are in God's world because He *wants* us to be here. See further Keith Ward *Why There Almost Certainly is a God*, (Oxford: Lion Hudson, 2009)

[116] 2 Cor. 5:17

[117] It took the Church almost 500 years to clarify its thinking about the Holy Trinity.

[118] Luke 19:10

[119] All three stories appear in Luke 15.

[120] 2 Cor. 5:17

[121] John 3:3

become aware of His Presence, we claim by faith that He knows us as His children, His friends. Being *found* is of course only the beginning; the relationship grows as it is fed through prayer.

God creates the experience of close friendship through prayer, the intimacy of parent and child. Through this "transforming conversation," God moulds us and shapes our characters. We experience changes in attitudes, our perspectives, and ourselves. This in turn will affect how we behave in God's world and the situations we can influence.

However, it is not difficult to let this relationship slip (from our side) as life happens, work or personal issues consume our time, and we either omit prayer or forget to pray altogether. We touched on this earlier in the book in the discussion around the "prompt to pray," thinking of this as an alarm bell sounding to warn that all is not well (in this case, in our relationship with God). Sir Jacob Astley before the Battle of Edgehill in the English Civil War famously prayed,

> Lord, You know I shall be very busy this day. If I forget You, please do not forget me.

God will never forget us, [122] and we will not forget Him when life gets in the way if our prayer life is grounded in personal habit and becomes part of our personal culture.

When Jesus taught His disciples to pray, He said they should pray that God's Kingdom would come[123]. Since then, every disciple, every follower of Jesus who prays the Lord's Prayer is joining in with this request. As we know, the Kingdom Jesus was talking about

---

[122] *'I will not forget you. See, I have inscribed you on the palms of my hands.'* Isaiah 49: 15,16
[123] Matthew 6:10

was not a place, not some far off country[124]. Instead, the Kingdom is a way of living. It starts with an acknowledgement that God is indeed Supreme Ruler, the Most High (despite every indication to the contrary). As human beings, we are to be His loyal subjects, His children, His friends. Jesus's first recorded words announced that the Kingdom had come[125], yet He later spoke about how there was more to come. Rather like the growing grain of mustard seed, or the yeast in the dough, the coming of God's Kingdom is about transformational change. So every time we pray "Your Kingdom Come" we are in fact praying for a wholesale transformation of ourselves and everything around us.

One day, when Jesus returns to reign in glory, God's Kingdom will come in all its fullness. In the meantime, His followers – you and me - are commissioned to partner with Him in this transformational work of bringing in the Kingdom. Through our intentional meetings with the living God in individual prayer, His priorities can become ours. The prayer connection helps in cultivating a "Kingdom perspective" so that we begin to look at the world (and ourselves) as it were through God's eyes and see where and how His Kingdom can come.

We have seen several examples in this book of how women and men have made a huge impression on the world around them as they have been energised and transformed by their relationship with God in prayer. For example, Amy Carmichael's world was turned upside down as she prayerfully reflected on her encounter with the poor woman in Belfast. As a result, she changed the futures for many Indian children for nearly half a century. Similarly, Beatrice Smith was not only able to survive the horrors of the Rwandan genocide but became a source of comfort and nurture for her family. Bob Pierce's "kingdom perspective" was born within his time of quiet

---

[124] John 19:36
[125] Mark 1:14

encounter with God in prayer. As a result, He saw what he could do to transform the situations of hugely disadvantaged children, Corrie Ten Boom, who said she learnt more about prayer in Ravensbruck concentration camp than anywhere else, drew her strength from God as she worked to bring about renewed hope for many whose lives had been dislocated by the Second World War. And Phil? His relationship problems with his in-laws took on a different shape in the light of a kingdom perspective. All these followers of Jesus were (and are) part of extending God's kingdom outside, in the world, or within themselves.

As I write, many Christians around the world are sharing again in the Archbishop of Canterbury's "Your Kingdom Come" prayer initiative. This is an invitation from Justin Welby to join in prayer – especially in the ten-day period between Ascension Day and Pentecost - that God's Kingdom, and His Holy Spirit, will come. In particular, the call is to pray for named individuals to come to know Jesus Christ. This call to prayer provides a renewed prompt to focus on specific people and situations. But it also invites us to look beyond, to try and imagine what it would *really* look like for God's Kingdom to come, and for His Holy Spirit to fall. We may then find ourselves praying beyond our comfort zone, beyond the familiar and what is known, and maybe even attempting new things for Him.

God invites us into relationship through prayer; He calls us to service; He asks that we are co-builders with Him of His Kingdom. He invites us to enjoy His Friendship and rejoice in His Fatherhood. He longs that we *pray*.

Jesus said,

> Listen! I am standing at the door and knocking; if you hear my voice and open the door, I will come in to you and eat with you, and you with me.[126]

---

[126] Rev. 3:20

Some Useful Prayer Websites

www.churchofengland.org/prayer-and-worship/join-us-in-daily -prayer

www.methodist.org.uk/our-faith/prayer/prayer-of-the-day

thedailyprayerblog.blogspot.com

www.sacredspace.ie

www.dailyprayer.us

www.prayer-coach.com

CPSIA information can be obtained
at www.ICGtesting.com
Printed in the USA
BVHW031407251120
594213BV00001B/72